'Even among WWII memoirs – a genre studded with extraordinary stories – this autobiography looms large, a work of exceptional substance and style . . . Armstrong and Opdyke demonstrate an almost uncanny power to place readers in the young Irene's shoes . . . Readers will be riveted – and no-one can fail to be inspired by Opdyke's courage.'

Publishers Weekly

'Opdyke's remarkable story is simply told, with clarity and feeling. Her enormous courage is all the more compelling because the events in her life are true, and her transformation from an innocent schoolgirl to a determined resistance fighter will inform and inspire readers.'

School Library Journal

'Opdyke tells her story in a voice that reflects the clarity and conviction of a woman to whom acts of heroism and courage are simply natural human responses to inhumanity. She uses simple and direct language to demystify the concept of heroism and depict courage as a matter of basic human decency well within the capability of ordinary humans.'

Washington Post

Selected as joint Best Autobiography in a *Publishers Weekly* poll of children's booksellers in 1999

Selected for the American Library Association Top Ten Best Books for Young Adults 2000

IN MY HANDS

Memories of a
Holocaust Rescuer

IN MY HANDS

Memories of a
Holocaust Rescuer

IRENE GUT OPDYKE *with*
Jennifer Armstrong

CORGI BOOKS

IN MY HANDS
A CORGI BOOK: 0 552 547166

First published in the United States of America
by Alfred A. Knopf, Inc, 1999
Published in Great Britain by Corgi

PRINTING HISTORY
Corgi edition published 2001

5 7 9 10 8 6 4

Set in 10½/14½ pt Bembo by Falcon Oast Graphic Art

Corgi Books are published by Random House Children's Books
61-63 Uxbridge Road, London W5 5SA,
a division of The Random House Group Ltd,
in Australia by Random House Australia (Pty) Ltd,
20 Alfred Street, Milsons Point, NSW 2061, Australia,
in New Zealand by Random House New Zealand Ltd,
18 Poland Road, Glenfield, Auckland 10, New Zealand
and in South Africa by Random House (Pty) Ltd,
Endulini, 5a Jubilee Road, Parktown 2193, South Africa.

Printed and bound in Great Britain by Clays Ltd, St Ives plc.

Irene Gut Opdyke wishes to express her thanks to
the following

To God, the creator of all living things

To Pastors Al and Loretta Forniss from my church, Desert
Bloom Ministries, for their love and support

To Jennifer Armstrong, Reverend Frank Eiklor of Shalom
International, Rabbi Haime Asa, Rabbi Harold M. Schulweis,
Father Karp of John Paul II Church, the United Jewish
Appeal, and the Simon Wiesenthal Center

Also to my daughter Janina, son-in-law Gary Smith,
grandchildren Ray and Robert, and to Larry, Lyn and
Josh Nantais for their continued love and help in my
endeavour to bring togetherness among all people

And to all the people in the churches, temples, and schools I
have spoken to, remember, 'Love, not Hate'

To my daughter, Janina

And for the young people, who can accomplish the impossible and can achieve greatness by finding the strength in God and in the goodness of the human spirit. I dedicate my life story to encourage them to find hope and strength within themselves. Courage is a whisper from above: when you listen with your heart, you will know what to do and how and when.

With all my life –

Irene Gut Opdyke

I dedicate this book with love and respect to Irene.

Jennifer Armstrong

contents

Tears

There was a bird flushed up from the wheat fields, disappearing in a blur of wings against the sun, and then a gunshot and it fell to the earth. But it was not a bird. It was not a bird, and it was not in the wheat field, but you can't understand what it was yet.

How can I tell you about this war? How can I say these things? If I tell you all at once – first this happened, and then this, and these people died and those people lived and then it was over – you will not believe me. Sometimes I wonder if these things could have happened. Was it me? Was that girl me? Was I really there? Did I see this happening? In the war, everything was unnatural and unreal. We wore masks and spoke lines that were not our own. This happened to me, and yet I still don't understand how it happened at all.

So I must tell you slowly. Slowly, and with everything fine and clear. I will start at the beginning, because it started long ago.

Before time, before there was a Poland, the trees wept as they fell into the Wisła. The great river carried the trees north into the Baltic and mingled their tears with the sea. Centuries passed, and the fishermen on the coast hunted the shoreline for those tears – they had become golden pearls of amber washed smooth by the waves. From Byzantium, from Rome, from the steppes, and from the Holy Land, the merchants came north for the amber that held the sun in its heart. Then the Teutonic Knights swept like a storm wave into Poland and took the amber trade prisoner. No-one could buy the gems except from these German knights, and Polish smugglers were put to death in the fortress of Malbork.

When the Germans stormed once more into Poland in 1939, we smuggled again. But this time it was not amber. They were tears of another sort.

I Was Almost Fast Enough

Lilac Time

Kozienice is a small village in eastern Poland. Here, on May Day, 1921, my mother went to the riverbank with her friends. It was dusk, and the breeze carried the scent of lilacs. The call of a cuckoo from the forest made the village girls laugh as they picked their way among the reeds and forget-me-nots at the water's edge, and the grasses brushed their ankles with dew as they passed. My mother carried a block of wood with her name written on it, Maria Rębieś. Also on the block of wood were a stub of candle and a small wreath of flowers.

Each of the laughing girls carried a block. Again the cuckoo called from the birch trees while Maria and her friends lit their candles. The smell of the matches and burning wax mingled with the scent of lilac. Clutching their skirts up around their knees, the girls waded into the chilly water to launch their boats. The fleet of candles drifted out into the current, turned and bobbed as though bowing farewell, and floated away.

Downriver were the young men, and among them was Władysław Gut, a young architect and chemist who was overseeing the construction of a nearby ceramics factory. He stood apart from the other young men on the riverbank, smoking a cigarette and watching as they joked and wrestled in the shallows.

Gut did not think, at first, that he would join the village men in their holiday game. The ancient folk customs of this rural countryside near the Ukrainian area of Poland seemed like relics of a long-ago century. But the twilight was deepening, and the laughter rose in excitement as the flock of candles came into view, floating beneath the slender green fingers of a willow. The lights were bewitching. Gut tossed his cigarette into the damp grass and walked nearer to the water to watch the May boats drift toward him. Swallows dipped and skimmed over the water and arced away.

The men were wading out now, teasing one another over their sweethearts, each one hoping to get the boat with her name on it. Gut bent quickly to unlace his boots and peel off his socks, and then waded into the water with the others, the hems of his city trousers clinging to his legs.

'How will you know which is Janka's boat, Tadek?' one man called.

'She promised to put only bluebells on it,' came a reply over the dark water.

'Did you hear that, Marek? Janka's boat has bluebells – if you want her that's the boat to catch!'

Gut stood with the stream coursing past his legs. In the darkness of the woods behind him, an owl hooted. The hairs on his arms rose at the cold and at the eeriness of the fairy lights that moved silently towards him. One boat floated apart from the others, farther out in the current. He felt carefully with his bare feet over the stones on the streambed and stepped out deep. Maria Rębieś' candle sailed straight into his outstretched hands, like a bird settling onto its nest.

I like to think of my parents meeting this way, to think of the sweet and happy years of Poland's independence between the wars. I like to think of the scent of lilacs luring my father into the water in his city clothes, and my mother in her white dress, sitting on the bank upstream with her knees tucked up under her chin, dreaming of the man who would catch her boat. They were married soon after, and I was born on May 5, in 1922, when the lilacs were blooming again.

We lived for my first year in Kozienice. Our house sat just above the river, and in the spring of my first year, the sound of the rushing water spoke to me through the open windows. While my mother was busy one morning, I made my baby way out of the house, toddling across the new grass to the water. Our dog, Myszka, followed. I tottered at the brink, watching the flashing water as it streamed past.

Then Myszka sank her teeth into my diaper and began tugging backward. Stubbornly, I tried to crawl forward to stare again into the water, but the dog would not let go. She also could not bark, so this tug-of-war went on for several minutes as I inched my way closer and closer to the edge.

Then, the silent voice that speaks in mothers' ears whispered to my mamusia. She looked out the window, and with a shriek she sped outside. 'Irena!' Gasping, she snatched me from the water's edge. Myszka collapsed on the ground, wagging her tail, as Mamusia praised and thanked her.

For several days, our heroic dog was the talk of Kozienice. Neighbours, friends, members of our church –

one by one they stopped by to marvel at little Myszka and stroke my baby face. The rabbi from Kozienice's synagogue came by to bless us both, and our priest took Mamusia's hands in both of his. 'God has plans for your daughter, Pani Gutowna. We must watch to see what little Irenka does.'

Father, or Tatuś, as I called him, thanked the priest and the rabbi, and said they would indeed expect much of me.

Over time, as we moved from Kozienice to Chelm to Radom and to Suchednów for Tatuś' job, one sister, then another, then another, and then another arrived, every two years or so, until there were five girls running and screaming around the house: Janina, Marysia, Bronia, Władzia, and me, Irena. Even our new dog, Lalka, was a female.

When my youngest sister, Władzia, was born, we moved to Częstochowa, northwest of Kraków. Thus, I spent several years living at the feet of the Black Madonna, the mother saint of Poland, who dwells in the shrine of Jasna Góra, the Bright Mountain fortress. Our home was next door to the church of St Barbara, and we had a clear view up the tree-lined avenue to Jasna Góra. Every year on the Virgin's important holy days, pilgrims would come from all over Poland to worship at the shrine. My first sister, Janina, and I would go outside to offer lemonade and water to the pilgrims, who made the final approach to the shrine on their knees.

We also lavished our tender, girlish care on wounded animals all the time. Cats, dogs, rabbits, birds – we brought our small patients home to Mamusia, who tended them expertly. The animals that could get better did, and we would let them go or find homes for them. The animals that could not get better died, and we held solemn burials in the backyard, in the shadow of St Barbara's lofty sanctuary. My mother once raised a baby blackbird we had found fallen from its nest, and it always lived nearby and would fly in through the open window when she whistled for it. One fall, when the storks began to migrate, we discovered a young stork with an injured wing who was trying to fly off with his fellows. He couldn't get off the ground, so we bundled our coats around him and took him home, being careful of his long, sharp beak.

'Mamusia, can you fix it?' I called as Janina and Marysia and I carried the lanky bird into the kitchen.

Mamusia and our hired girl, Magda, were chopping cabbage for pickles. Mamusia turned around, wiping her hands on a towel. Her eyebrows went up in surprise at the ungainly creature standing before her, blinking its black button eyes and clacking its yellow beak against the back of a chair. It had a strong wild smell of mud. While Janina and Marysia and I watched, Mamusia flexed the stork's wing and then began to bandage it.

'What will you call him?' Magda asked us as our mother worked.

'Bociek,' Marysia piped up. 'Can we keep him, Mamusia?'

'He cannot go south with his friends this winter,' our mother said. 'But you cannot keep a big stork in the house. He might be dangerous, and we do not want him to lose his wildness. He should rejoin the other storks in the spring when they return. Put him in the cellar.'

'I can catch frogs for him,' Janina said.

'Me, too,' I said. 'And fish. We'll make him strong.'

'You might have to feed him mice when the winter comes and the water freezes,' Mamusia said.

Janina and Marysia and I all pulled faces at that. Bociek bobbed his head as though agreeing, and then dabbled with his beak at his new bandage.

The door to the dining room opened, and the little ones, Bronia and Władzia, peeked in. Bronia stared at Bociek. She stared at Władzia. The girls backed out and the door swung shut.

We moved Bociek into the cellar and kept him fed and warm. As the winter descended on Poland, many other birds flew south to escape the cold. And then the snow came.

The winters in Poland are very long and very bitter, but in our house, we were always warm and happy. After dinner, we gathered around the piano to sing folk songs while Tatuś played.

Other nights, Mamusia would welcome her friends into the house for feather stripping. The women would sit around the table, peeling the soft fluff from duck and goose quills, and tell ghost stories while they stuffed pillows. Janina and I would sneak down the stairs to listen to their tales. The air would fill with floating down like softly falling snow and Janina and I would press our faces into our laps to muffle our sneezes.

Then, as the winter deepened, it would be time to think of Christmas. We spread the table with hay, to signify the manger, and then laid a fresh white cloth over it. All day long on Christmas Eve, we were busy in the kitchen, making pierogis, breads, cookies, pickled fish, potatoes, and cabbage. We would laugh and sing 'Bóg Się Rodzi' and other carols as the house filled with the scent of vanilla, cinnamon, and mushrooms.

When night fell, we bundled ourselves into our coats and hats, and stepped outside to walk to the shrine of Jasna Góra. The snow squeaked under our boots as we tramped toward the Bright Mountain fortress. I imagined the Holy Mother appearing over the fortress as she had when the invading Swedes had conquered all of Poland, and the last of the defenders were making their stand at Jasna Góra. It was said that her divine image had shielded the fortress from harm, allowing Jasna Góra to withstand the siege and throw back the invaders.

I tipped my head back and looked at the stars glittering in the frozen sky. No Holy Mary appeared to me, but the lights pouring from the windows of the fortress on the hill were a wonderful vision in themselves. With the other pilgrims, we wound our way, singing, up the hillside to the magnificent basilica. Inside the church, the high, vaulted ceiling echoed with song and prayer. The flickering light of a thousand candles gleamed on holy relics and statues. And behind the altar, revealed behind its wooden door, was the Black Madonna of Częstochowa.

I was always awed when I saw the holy icon. It was a small painting, and it was dark with age. But the simple image of the Madonna and Child was said to have miraculous power, and on Christmas night, with the stuffy air full of incense and the voices of the priests murmuring in Latin, on that night it was possible to believe the painting was miraculous, that it was the protector of Poland. It was easy for me to believe that with such a powerful guardian, Poland would never fall.

This was in the early 1930s, when it was still possible to believe such things.

Before the Storm

In 1934, German president Paul von Hindenburg died. By August, Adolf Hitler had become both chancellor and president of Germany, taking the title *Der Führer*. I was oblivious to politics, however; if, some evening over cigarettes and vodka, Tatuś and his partner discussed the rise of Hitler and his fanatical cronies in neighbouring Germany, I did not pay attention.

My teenage years had begun, and we now lived in the small town of Kozłowa Góra, in the Polish district known as Upper Silesia, or Oberschlesien. Here, we were only six kilometres from the German border, and many of our new neighbours were of German descent. We began to learn German in school, and grew accustomed to seeing it written in town and hearing it spoken on the street. People came and went easily across the border, especially in the countryside, and there were some little towns that had never quite made up their minds whether they were Polish or German. Indeed, the borders had shifted so often over the centuries that to many people, it did not make any difference whether they were governed from Berlin or Warsaw.

Because of our name, Gut, many people assumed that we were of German descent, but my parents were fiercely patriotic. We were Polish. I was raised to be proud of that fact. Lessons in school had told me the cruel history of my country, which had been invaded repeatedly over the centuries – from the west by the Germans, from the north by Swedes and Lithuanians, from the east by Tatars and Russians, from the south by Hungarians. Always, Poland had struggled to preserve itself. Its borders had shifted over the centuries and sometimes dissolved altogether as it was sucked in by a larger or fiercer power. Beautiful, bountiful Poland, a country whose very name means 'field', had the richest agricultural land in Europe, and every other country wanted to reap that harvest. We Poles knew we were surrounded by grasping hands; the knowledge made us guard our land and our identity all the more loyally.

But as I say, I was a teenager, and politics was abstract to me. Also, the subject was never discussed at dinner – in those days, it was not a suitable topic for girls. Besides, I was busy with other things. In high school, I became a member of the school dance group, and we performed traditional Polish dances at festivals all over the western and southern part of the country.

Performing with the dance group gave me a taste of the spotlight, and I began to try out for school plays. Sometimes I actually daydreamed about being a movie actress, but I was secretly afraid that I was too plain. I was thin and pale; often, on the way to school, I tried to darken my eyebrows with burnt matches and put some colour in my cheeks and lips with red paper that I dampened with spit. But as my sisters and I grew older, it became clear that although I was the eldest, Janina was the standout. She was taller than I was, elegant and graceful. She turned heads wherever she went, and I always seemed to be in her shadow, the ugly duckling.

I did not worry, particularly. At that time, I was not interested in boys, except as friends. I wore my hair short, and climbed trees and rode horses and made up adventure stories that I wrote down in my diary. In my fantasies, I was always caught up in heroic struggles, and I saw myself saving lives, sacrificing myself for others. I had far loftier ambitions than mere romance.

One Christmas, I became convinced these fantasies would come true. My grandmother Rębieś had taught us an old custom: we melted candle wax and poured it into a bowl of very cold water. The moment the wax hit the water it hardened into a twisted, fantastical shape, and we tried to read our fortunes by holding the blob of wax up against the light and seeing what sort of shadow it cast. When it came to my turn, I held my wax up to the light and we all studied the silhouette on the wall. It resembled a ship crossing the ocean, we decided. A ship with a crucifix on its prow. My sisters were awed into silence by this fortune, and I was thrilled: I was destined to have adventures. Righteous adventures.

However, in Kozłowa Góra in the mid-thirties, there weren't very many righteous adventures available. Mamusia urged us to direct our energy into useful – although unexciting – projects. Along with my sisters, I helped her prepare baskets of food for the poor and the sick. We scavenged in the ash heap at Tatuś' glass and ceramics factory, looking for rejects of coloured glass. We gave these to women who crushed them into fake gems for decorating picture frames. In every charitable act we performed, Mamusia and Tatuś were our models; they were generous and kind to everyone, even to the Gypsies who camped in the woods outside town and made people suspicious with their strange costumes and language. Wounded animals, out-of-luck neighbours, sick strangers – Mamusia and Tatuś welcomed them all.

With their encouragement, I decided to become a volunteer for the Red Cross, and I donned the uniform of a candy striper. At our candy striper meetings, we practised bandaging one another, learning first aid, and preparing ourselves for unspecified emergencies. We visited the hospital, bringing flowers and fruit to the patients and trying to be helpful. It was in the hospital that I began to admire the nuns who had devoted their lives to the sick. Over time, I concluded that I should be a nun. It was not the nuns' life of piety that attracted me, but their sense of purpose and their devotion to service.

Tatuś was surprised when I told him. He suggested that I first train as a nurse. If that did not satisfy me, then I could begin studying to become a nun. I would enroll in the nursing school of St Mary's Hospital, in Radom. It was over two hundred kilometres away, but it was the best nursing school in Poland.

So, in 1938, I began my studies in Radom. The city was an industrial centre filled with munitions plants, enamel works, steel foundries, ceramics factories, and tanneries, which filled the smoky air with a rank, animal-chemical smell. I lived in a rooming house with other student nurses, and threw myself into my work. I missed my family, and I was nervous to be in a strange city, so I hid behind my books and studied hard to forget my loneliness. Most of the other girls took their duties lightly, and went out in the evenings to the movies or to dances. But I took my responsibilities very seriously and, being shy, I shunned their company. My mother's sister, Helen, lived in Radom, and I sometimes had dinner with her; but for the most part, when I was not at school or in the hospital I stayed in my room and studied anatomy or chemistry. I intended to be the best in my class and make my parents proud of me.

The practical experience I gained in the hospital taught me many things that weren't in my books. One thing I learned on my rounds was that men love to make young nurses blush, and I came to dread entering the men's wards. Winks and grins and requests for baths sometimes brought such colour into my face that the men would howl with laughter and tease me even more. I was only sixteen, after all, and I was as easy to startle and flush from cover as a pheasant.

As evening fell, most of the girls in my rooming house would chatter and laugh as they went out, leaving the house quiet in their wake. I was happy to stay alone. From my window as I studied, I sometimes saw groups of university students walking arm in arm in the glare of the streetlights, singing patriotic songs, their coats flapping open in the breeze. I was beginning to be aware that Hitler had made threats against Poland. Under the Treaty of Versailles, which had settled the Great War of 1914–1918, Germany had lost much territory that it had won in earlier conquests. Now Hitler was determined to reclaim that land, to revive the power and might of Germany and make it great once more in the eyes of the world.

But much of the land Hitler wanted was Poland's, and

always had been. Many German immigrants had settled there, especially in the west, where my family was, but that did not make it Germany! Hitler wanted *Lebensraum*, living space, for the Germans, and our Poland was the space he wanted.

'Irena, we want you to come home,' Tatuś and Mamusia wrote to me in their letters. 'Many people think war is imminent, and we hate to think of you so far from us. The family should be together.'

But I did not listen. If it came to war, I would do my part for Poland. If it came to war, my country would need trained nurses. No, I wrote to my parents. I must stay here. I know what my duty is. If Hitler tries to come here, we will fight him and we will chase him all the way back to Berlin. Besides, we knew that old enemies Germany and the Soviet Union watched each other like two dogs guarding a bone; if one of them made the slightest move toward Poland, it would be considered an act of war against the other. The mutual suspicion and hatred between the Germans and the Soviets was our guarantee.

When I returned home for the summer at the end of my first year, I found Kozłowa Góra had changed. Many of our neighbours had become German, renouncing their Polish heritage, speaking only German, openly admiring the policies of Hitler and his National Socialist party, the Nazis. And in some shops – not many, but some – there were signs saying, 'Don't Buy from Jews!' or 'A Poland Free from Jews Is a Free Poland.'

This mystified me. In my home, there had never been any distinction made between people. Many of our friends were Jewish, but we did not say to ourselves, 'Our Jewish friends, the Gonsiorowiczes.' It had never occurred to me to distinguish between people based on their religion. But this was precisely what Hitler was doing a mere six kilometres away.

We did not imagine where it would lead. How could we? To us, Germany had always been a seat of civilization, the home of poets and musicians, philosophers and scientists. We believed it was a rational, cultured country.

How could we know that the Germans did not feel the same about us? How could we know the depth of their scorn for us? Despite our centuries of glorious achievements, despite our Chopins and Copernicuses, our cathedrals and our heroes and our horses – despite all this, Germany viewed Poland as a land of Slavic brutes, fit only for labour.

And so Hitler wanted to destroy us.

The Lightning War

That summer after my first year of school was the last happy time I was to spend with my family, but none of us knew it in August when I returned to Radom to resume my studies. On the twenty-fourth, Germany and the Soviet Union stunned the world by announcing the Molotov-Ribbentrop Pact, a non-aggression treaty: neither would make war against the other. People gathered on the streets and in the cafés, speculating about what this news meant to Poland. We sat defenceless between these two countries: would they simply carve us up and eat us? There was no topic of conversation besides politics.

Suspense grew, and the heat was sweltering. I kept a basin of water on my desk at night so I could wipe down my face and arms and neck while I studied in my hot, stuffy room. The rattle of trucks and cars reached me through my open window, and the smell of exhaust fumes, and the sour breath of a cheap restaurant next door. As the month ran out, all of us began to look toward the sky, thirsty for rain. Dust rose from the roads as we walked from our dormitory to St Mary's. In the pastures on the edge of town, horses pawed at the hard, baked ground. It was the kind of dry, oppressive heat that comes before a thunderstorm.

On September 1, the storm broke, but not in the way we had expected. I was on my way to the hospital, walking across an empty lot, when a steady, pulsing drone reached my ears. I looked up, one hand on my Red Cross cap to keep it from slipping as I tipped my head back. Before I even saw the planes, I began to hear explosions, and then there they were – the sky was black with them: row after row of German bombers, flying in formation over Radom. Even as I covered my ears against the roar, I felt the earth shaking with detonations. Across the field from where I stood, the front of an apartment building suddenly sheared away, and a blue plush sofa toppled to the street. Dust and smoke billowed up from every corner of the city. I stood frozen, too stunned to move. The air was filled with the screams of falling bombs and the roar of their blasts. Sirens wailed from every direction.

'Get down, you idiot!' someone screamed at me. 'You're going to get yourself killed!'

I felt someone catch my arm and drag me toward a ditch. In a daze, I looked to see who was with me; it was one of the interns from St Mary's, Dr Gribowski. We crouched in the ditch as the German planes charged by overhead. With each bomb blast, my whole body jumped. Clumps of dirt rained down on my head, and a sharp chip of masonry cut my cheek. From nearby I heard the terrified scream of a horse, and then the crashing of glass and an engine racing, and all the time the sound of the airplane engines kept pounding against our ears.

'Come on!' Gribowski shouted. 'They'll need us at the hospital.'

Together, we began dodging across the lot. Craters filled with bricks and rubble blocked our way as we bolted into a street. The city was on fire. People were running wildly, screaming for their children, screaming from terrible wounds. A toddler whose face was streaked with dirt and tears sat naked on a set of front steps; behind him was only empty space where a house should have been. A truck barrelled down the street, honking its horn continuously; it crashed into a lamp-post, reversed, and jolted off again. I jerked at another huge explosion from the direction of the munitions factory. As I stumbled along the sidewalk I saw a woman whose hands were covered with blood, and I opened my mouth to say something but could not speak. A dog was barking, barking.

'The hospital!' the intern yelled. The sirens shrieked like lunatics. I thought I would begin screaming myself at any moment.

St Mary's was in chaos when we arrived. Plaster dust rained down from the ceiling with each blast, and the lights swung wildly, throwing weird shadows across the wards. Doctors and nurses barked orders over the moans of patients. Nuns sped from one bed to another, their black habits billowing around them. And the wounded – the wounded were everywhere, on beds, on chairs, on the floor, holding themselves up against the walls, crowding the stairwells. I hurried into a surgery ward and my foot slid out from under me; I looked down, and saw a smear of blood on the floor. It was unreal – one minute I had been home in the shelter of my loving family and the next I was standing in blood and ducking at the whistle of a bomb. This could not be me!

'Irena Gutowna, we need you over here!' someone shouted.

My whole world was now St Mary's Hospital. I slept in

my clothes, huddled under a sink or inside a broom closet, flinching at every loud noise. The rest of the time was one grotesque emergency after another. We were out of food, now we were out of sulpha drugs, we had no clean sheets, now the electricity was out – and the wounded kept arriving. In addition to civilians, we soon had Polish soldiers in the hospital, and from them we began to hear reports of the ground invasion.

German tanks had rolled over the border by the thousands. The ground, baked hard by summer sun, made roads unnecessary: the Panzers simply rolled over the amber fields, threshing the harvest to dust. Behind the tanks came the trucks and the infantry, the Wehrmacht, attacking Polish soldiers and civilians alike, pounding cities and villages to ruins. It was total war, war unlike anything we'd ever heard of. The carnage was staggering. Germany had claimed western Poland, chewed it up, and swallowed it in one gulp.

My hands shook as I tried to apply dressings to terrible wounds. My family was in the west. Kozłowa Góra, only six kilometres from the old border, was now trapped inside Hitler's Germany. With phone service out, I had no way to contact Tatuś and Mamusia. I had no way of knowing if they were safe, if my sisters were alive and unhurt. I worked in a daze of grief for Poland and for myself. I feared I would never see my beloved family again. I thought briefly of my aunt Helen, wondering if I could get word to her, or if she was even there. Her husband was in the army, and who could say where he was now?

As the German divisions pressed toward Radom, the Polish army units, shockingly outgunned, began to retreat, and at St Mary's the army officers asked for nurses and doctors to accompany them. Without hesitation, I raised my hand to volunteer: I wanted to take part in driving the Germans out of my country.

'Hurry up, then,' one officer said as he checked his pistol. 'We're leaving now.'

I followed the group out to the alley, where the trucks were waiting. It was the first time I had set foot outside the hospital in four days, and I felt a strange disbelief that the sky was still blue and the sun was shining. Around me was complete destruction: cars burning, houses in ruins, glass and bricks strewn across the streets, a haze of smoke slinking along the sidewalks. Yet overhead were white, gauzy clouds. It was as though the sun and the clouds did not care that Poland was being murdered. I ducked into the back of a Red Cross truck filled with wounded soldiers, and gripped the tailgate as the truck lurched forward.

It seemed all Radom was fleeing the Germans. The roads were choked with cars and trucks, horse-drawn wagons, bicycles, people on foot pushing wheelbarrows. Our driver honked the horn, trying to get through the crowds on the main road east. We had forty kilometres to travel before we reached the Wisła River.

'We're going to blow the bridge once we get over,' I heard one soldier say to another. 'We can't let the Germans cross the Wisła.'

I stared out at the fleeing citizens, the evacuees, as we passed. I did not ask how they would get over the river. Their faces retreated from me, rushing backward as our truck hurried down the road, and in each face I saw Tatuś or Mamusia, Janina, Marysia, Bronia, or Władzia. I closed my eyes, desperate to stop them all from flying away from me. The tailpipe coughed exhaust fumes up into the open back of the truck, making my head swim and making me close my eyes even tighter. Then a wounded soldier cried out as we went over a bump, and I had to force myself to help him. The kilometres passed by in a blur of abandoned fields and empty houses. The road was littered with discarded suitcases, broken-down cars, piles of bedding.

On the edge of a field I saw a peasant's cottage, its door open. Once, as a child, I had visited a farm outside Radom. It had a house like this one, with timber walls painted bone white, and a thatched roof. We had gone on a Sunday in the spring, when the farmer was taking down the bales of hay he had mounded around his house for winter insulation. As he pulled down the hay, scores of mice that had been nesting inside all winter scattered in every direction, squeaking frantically, while the farmer's sons chased them and killed them with sticks. I had stood shuddering with horror as the mice fled their home – that was like what I was watching now, but this was on such a large scale that I could not take it in. I could not believe what I was seeing.

Ahead there was shouting, and the din of many vehicles blaring their horns at once. Many kilometres behind us, in the direction of Radom, we heard the thunder of tank fire. The sky behind us was thick with smoke. Our truck ground to a halt, but the engine shivered and shook like a terrified animal. We heard yelling, and then a cavalry officer galloped past us, away from the bridge, sabre held aloft.

'What does he think he'll do, attack a tank like that?' a soldier beside me wondered.

The truck jerked forward again, and I saw the stone

parapets of the bridge as we began to cross the river. The Wisła churned below us, gunmetal grey, and the bloated body of a horse turned and rolled in the current. It had no head. I closed my eyes as my stomach heaved, and when we bumped off the end of the bridge on the eastern shore I heard the footsteps of soldiers running back to lay explosives. Our truck whined and ground through gears up a rise, and then picked up speed. As we crested the hill, we heard the dull boom of the bridge being blown. I don't think any of us really believed that it would stop the Germans, but we pretended we did. We boasted that Hitler would drown in Mother Wisła, that Poland's great river would rise up in a flood to stop the enemy's advance. But even as we did, we heard the drone of Luftwaffe airplanes again, and we had to swallow our cheers.

We drove for hours, until we reached another hospital. I don't even know where it was. I was so tired that I fell asleep in the truck as the wounded were being unloaded, but by then there were shouts of warning – the Germans had brought pontoons, and were already bridging the Wisła. The doctors were cursing, some even crying, as they ordered the wounded soldiers back onto the trucks.

'Where are we going now?' I asked one of the soldiers.

'Train station. We'll try to get northeast, to Kovno.'

The sun was bleeding into the western hills, and it was already dark in the northeast, where Polish Lithuania stretched up toward Russia. I clutched at the side of the truck as we jounced down the road to the train station, and when we got nearer I saw that there were broken-down military transports straddling the tracks. Soldiers were hacking down saplings and chopping the branches from large trees to drape over the train cars for camouflage. An officer stood on the station platform yelling, 'A doctor! Where's a damned doctor!'

For a moment, the storm of frantic activity halted. We all turned our heads to listen, and we heard again the pulsing drone of approaching bombers.

'These are Red Cross trucks!' I said to no-one in particular. I grabbed a nurse's arm. 'We're marked with red crosses – they won't bomb us, will they?'

'I don't know, dear. Help me with this man.'

I turned to help her support a soldier with a broken leg through the station, but my heart was racing as the sound of the planes grew louder. There were soldiers trying to push the broken trucks off the train tracks, and a young doctor was yelling for someone to bring water for washing, he had to perform surgery, and the train engineer was shouting to a brake-man on the carriage behind him as bursts of steam billowed out around the wheels, and then the bombs began falling on us, whistling as they came.

Instantly, the shingled roof of the station burst into flame, and the spruce trees on the other side of the tracks flared up like candles. The planes were dropping incendiary bombs, which burned right through the metal roof over the platform. I could not catch my breath even to scream. The other nurse and I dragged and pushed the soldier between us up onto the train steps and into the carriage. The moment we were inside, the nurse left me with the wounded soldier and ran back for another.

He had his arm thrown across my shoulder, and his weight dragged me down. 'Here, rest here,' I whispered, trying to prop him up against the wall of the train compartment. His face was colourless, and shiny with sweat.

'Are you a nurse?' he gasped, trying to wet his lips. His gaze flicked to my Red Cross armband and then to my face. 'You look twelve years old.'

'I'm a student nurse, I'm seventeen,' I quavered. Then another bomb fell outside the carriage and the window shattered from the pelting shrapnel, and we both ducked flying glass.

I stood upright, clasping my hands together to keep them from shaking. On all sides, wounded soldiers lay or sat on the seats, moaning in pain. 'I'll get a doctor,' I said, as calmly as I could. 'I'll find a doctor. There must be a doctor on this train.'

There was a blast from the train's whistle and the chuff-chuff of the engine reached our ears through the crashing of bombs and the screams of men outside. I grabbed the door frame to keep myself steady as the train shuddered and began to move forward, taking us east – toward the Russians.

Mother Russia

Kovno was quiet. We were far from the fighting, deep in the Lithuanian section of Poland, near the border with the Soviet Union. We were about two hundred altogether, soldiers, officers, and medical staff. We huddled in our coats outside one of the military warehouses. I had no gloves, and had to blow on my hands in the early-morning chill. We had left summer behind us. One of my nails had been torn almost to the quick, and it stung sharply as I blew on my fingers.

I had no idea what was going on or what would happen. I was the youngest member of the group, and nobody bothered to explain anything to me. There was a general, whose name I never learned. I knew we were waiting for him to make an announcement. The soldiers were waiting to hear how the Polish army would make its stand. We only had to regroup and resupply, the officers were assuring their men, and then we would be ready to confront the Germans. We would show the Wehrmacht what the Polish army was made of.

One man jerked his chin toward the door, and we all turned to see the general coming out with an aide by his side. They stood on the steps. In the crowd, the soldiers stood at attention. The walking wounded tried to square their shoulders or hold themselves straight, but too many of them were weak and fell back on their crutches. I and the other nurses stood in a group, hugging ourselves for warmth, waiting for the general to speak. I could see he had not shaved in a few days, and the stubble of whiskers on his chin and cheeks was white, making him look like a tired old man.

At last he cleared his throat. 'God will surely bless you all for the courage and strength you have shown. You have fought bravely for our beloved country. Your grandchildren will bless you for it.' Here he paused, and cleared his throat again. 'But the Polish army is through. I have just learned that the Germans and the Soviets have divided Poland between them. Even now, we are standing in Soviet territory. We are not a country any longer. There is no more Poland.'

Moans of dismay and cries of denial rose from the crowd. I looked at the nurse standing next to me. Tears were running down her face. I could not understand what the general meant. How could there not be a Poland anymore? My feet were on the ground, Polish ground. How could the land not be?

'The Polish government has reached England, and from there they will do everything possible to regain our country. In the meantime, you are free to go – to fight in the forests, to return to your homes—' His voice broke. Men throughout the crowd were crying now, cursing and sobbing at the same time. A colonel ripped the insignia from his uniform and crushed it in his hand, shaking with tears.

The general indicated the warehouse door. 'Take what you need. Take it all.' He pulled himself upright, and saluted the company. His chin was trembling. Then he strode down the steps, the aide hurrying behind him.

At once, there was pandemonium. Everyone began talking, cursing the Germans and the Russians, trying to decide what to do. Some of the soldiers flung open the warehouse door, and within minutes, there was a steady stream of people going in and out. Blankets, guns, clothes, bottles of vodka, bags of flour, canned meat, cartons of cigarettes – anything useful was loaded onto the trucks we had commandeered. Someone dropped a bottle, and it smashed on the steps; a truck engine backfired as it roared to life. People were heading for the forest with everything they could carry.

And I was going, too. Somehow, I was going with the ragtag army-without-a-country into the Lithuanian forest. It seemed unreal to me, as though I were only acting a part in a play. This could not be me, climbing into a truck and sitting on a crate of ammunition. The real Irena belonged at home, not here, unwashed, hungry, shivering. I watched a louse crawl out of my coat sleeve. This was not really me with lice. It could not be.

The first night in the forest, we rigged blankets into tents. Some of us slept in the trucks, and some on the ground. Some didn't sleep at all, but stayed awake in the dark, smoking, plotting revenge. A few men got very drunk, and I heard them cursing and sobbing, or stumbling through their prayers. In the morning, we discovered that eight soldiers and officers had killed themselves during the night: guns in the mouth, knives across the throat.

That was how our first day as exiles in our own land began. Someone offered a plan; some of the men formed a committee of leadership, but I didn't know them and they never asked my opinion. We would head south, toward Lvov, over five hundred kilometres away.

Rumours constantly passed back and forth across our camp as we prepared to move: there was a general in Lvov – no, but there were five army units there and they were preparing to move against the Germans – no, but in Lvov there was an undersecretary of the Polish government and he was rallying the troops around him on orders from the exiled government in London – no, but in Lvov there would be an airlift of weapons and ammunition from the French – no, I never knew exactly why we were going to Lvov. Perhaps several of the men in charge had families there, and wanted to go home. I was put in a truck with the rest of the baggage, and we began our move.

We didn't know what to expect from the Lithuanians, who were closer in culture to the Russians than to the Poles. Now that we were an illegal army in Russian-held territory, we did not know if we were safe or not, if we would be welcomed by the locals. We made our way from one village to the next through the massive forest, trading our supplies for theirs: vodka for potatoes, tobacco for sausages, sugar for eggs. Some of the villagers met us with suspicion. Some shut their doors in our faces. Some made hard bargains. Others were good to us, and told us when there were Soviet troops nearby. We crossed into the Polish Ukraine, and I gathered nuts and mushrooms, as though in a caricature of my school outings. I found grapevines draped shroudlike over a tree, but the grapes were shrivelled and rotten from the frost. One afternoon as I walked the edge of a wood, there was an explosion of wing-beats at my feet, and a fat bird toiled upward, disappearing for a moment against the sun. Then there was a gunshot, and it fell to earth. One of the soldiers ran past me, grabbed up the bird, and wrung its neck for good measure. As he turned he saw my look, saw how I stared at him, saw me clutching the lapels of my coat together at my throat and breathing hard with surprise and remorse at having flushed the bird.

The fall turned into winter, and we drove past frozen marshes, along rivers crusted with ice, always taking refuge in the forests. We were like animals, scavenging to survive. We lived however we could, growing sick, shivering, huddling ourselves against the snow. I was anaemic, I knew; often I was so weak I felt faint if I stood up too quickly from scooping a handful of nuts from the ground. Sometimes we camped in one area for days, casting about like so many blind people, trying to learn what news there was. Other times we moved every day, testing first one Ukrainian village and then another for haven, without finding any.

Every hour, every minute we spent on the roads in our trucks, we were in danger. Members of our group developed strange rituals and superstitions, or carried good-luck charms. Our existence was so precarious that we had reverted to the ways of a more primitive time. Our fires were small, for fear of giving away our position to Russian patrols, and for the same reason we could not rally ourselves with singing. I stayed with the women, sunk in despair of ever seeing my family again. Christmas came and went without comment, and we entered 1940 without hope. The great reason for going to Lvov never materialized. I had no idea what we were doing or where we were going, and I don't believe anyone else did, either. We seemed to be caught in a useless orbit around Lvov, never making any definitive move.

In early January, I was chosen to go on a bartering mission with four soldiers and two other nurses. It was night, and the wheels of our truck churned through a dense layer of new snow. We parked in the woods at the edge of a village near Lvov and proceeded on foot. There were always Russian patrols around, so these missions were dangerous. My companions left me standing watch on a street corner while they entered a dark house.

I pressed my back against the building. The wind shoved against me, seeping through my thin coat. The cold came up through the soles of my boots, gripping my feet hard. I was so full of fear that it was hard to think. The Russians were Communists – they did not believe in God. I had no idea what they were like, or what it meant that they were now our masters, or what they would do if they found us. Overhead were stars, thousands of stars like a field of snowdrops in spring. I had the sensation that I sometimes had in the spring when I looked out over a meadow full of flowers that if I could only run fast enough I would rise up and fly. I wanted to run. I wanted my mother.

Through the clear, cold air came the sound of a truck, and I saw the beams of headlights bouncing down the street: a Russian patrol. My eyes turned toward the stars again for a moment, and then I was running from cover, trying to run fast enough to rise up into the night sky. I heard the voices of the Russian soldiers as they chased after me, their boots crunching in the snow. Ahead of me was the dark edge of the forest. My breath burned my throat, and I felt the sting of snow as it sifted into the tops of my boots. The Russian soldiers were behind me, yelling and laughing. I was a bird, and I was trying to fly off; and they were going to shoot me.

I was almost fast enough. I was almost fast enough.

The Hospital

This is hard to say. I was seventeen. I was shy with men; I had never had a boyfriend, never been kissed, I was a good Catholic girl. The Russian soldiers did not shoot me; they caught me and beat me unconscious. Then they raped me and left me for dead in the snow, under the frozen stars, with the dark forest keeping watch over my death.

But I did not die. Another patrol found me crumpled on the ground like a tinker's rag and threw me into the back of a truck. I flickered in and out of consciousness as the truck pounded over the hard roads. Then I was dragged out, and there were lights around me, and I was on a stretcher. A woman spoke to me gently in Russian, stroking my battered face, testing my limbs for fractures. 'Mamusia,' I whimpered, a child, and faded away again.

When I awoke I was in a bed, covered with blankets. I stared at the ceiling through swollen eyelids. I heard the windowpanes rattling. There was a storm outside, and the moaning of the wind echoed in my head. Slowly, I turned my head, and saw a young man and an older woman in a Russian uniform.

'I will interpret for the doctor,' the man said to me in Polish. 'Can you speak?'

I murmured something, and then cleared my throat. 'Yes.'

'You are in a hospital, but you are a prisoner. This is Dr Olga Pavlovskaya. What is your name?'

'Irena Gutowna.'

'Your age?'

'Seventeen.'

'Why were you in the forest?'

As I answered, he translated into Russian for the woman beside him. 'I was with the Polish medical corps. We – we went into the forest when we learned that Poland had been . . . that Poland was divided. We were trying to stay alive.'

Dr Pavlovskaya watched me intently as I spoke, a small frown creasing the skin between her eyebrows. She spoke in Russian.

'Are you a nurse?' the interpreter asked.

I stared at the ceiling again. I had deserted my post; my compatriots were gone, and now my body hurt everywhere. The memory of the soldiers' attack came over me in waves, and tears rolled down the sides of my face.

Again, 'Are you a nurse?'

'I'm a student nurse,' I whispered.

After the man spoke to Dr. Pavlovskaya, we were all silent for a moment, listening to the storm shake the building. Sleet rattled suddenly against the window like a handful of tiny bones. Then the doctor picked up my chart, read it over quickly, and spoke to the interpreter.

'There is no permanent damage, although it will take you some time to heal. You're malnourished and run-down, but I think within a few days you will be well enough to perform some light duties in the hospital. We are short-staffed now. I'll get you a hospital uniform when you are feeling better.'

I felt heavy and dull. The interpreter's voice faded as I fell into sleep. 'Where am I?' I tried to ask, but no words came out and I was gone.

Dr Pavlovskaya was there when I woke again the following afternoon. When she noticed me watching her, she gave me a swift, friendly smile, and spoke in Russian. Then she brushed my hair back from my face and took my wrist to check my pulse, murmuring a word that sounded like 'bird'. I closed my eyes, grateful for the kindness. Her hands were cool and soft. Then she left, and a nurse came to my bed with a basin and a clean hospital gown. I pulled myself painfully up in bed, holding myself like a sheet of glass. I swung my legs over the side, and my knees trembled when I stood, but I shook my head when the nurse offered to help me. I turned away to hide my bruised body from her gaze, and washed quickly, trying not to look myself. Then I dressed myself in the gown, and she motioned for me to follow her.

She led me down a long corridor in the hospital. It was filled with the familiar scents of chloroform and sickness. At a nurses' station, two women bickered over a chart, and then stared at me curiously as I passed. A cold draft blew across my ankles as I followed the nurse to a separate wing. Signs in Russian were posted on every door, and a photograph of Joseph Stalin brooded at the end of the corridor.

The rooms of the nurses' dormitory were all in a line, with a door on each end, making it necessary to walk through one room to get to another. We entered a room with three beds, and the nurse indicated the one that was mine. I sat uncertainly on the edge, and without further explanation, she left the way we had come.

I sat, trembling slightly with cold and with nervousness. Under the other two beds were trunks. A sweater was tossed over one of the beds, and a magazine lay facedown on the other. Still trembling, I crawled under the covers and rolled into a ball, hugging my knees to my chest. I wanted to sleep, to forget. I slept, but I could not forget.

I met my roommates the next day. They came in together, chatting tiredly, as though they had just gone off shift. One was tall, black-haired, and delicate. The other was coarser, with strong features. They sat on their beds and looked at me while they changed out of their uniforms.

The shorter one spoke in a loud, impatient voice; pointing to herself; she said, 'Galla', and then, pointing at the taller girl, 'Maruszka'.

'Irena,' I whispered.

They continued to talk, and once in a while, a word sounded familiar, close to a Polish word, and that began my education in Russian. I spent a few more days recovering and picking up bits of Russian from my roommates, and from then on, I was thrown into hospital work, often working alongside Galla and Maruszka. We started with common hospital words – bed, dressing, thermometer, blood – and went on with verbs, numbers, adjectives. In the dining hall that echoed with voices, I learned the names for fork, knife, potato, bread, tea, table. Within a few days, I was stumbling through short sentences in Russian, and Maruszka patiently read me the Moscow newspapers, simplifying the language as she went.

The papers trumpeted the Red Army's iron-fisted campaign on the Finnish border and its triumph over the

Polish resistance. I listened mutely to the reports about the defeated Polish army. I could not bear to think about it. I tried not to think about my family, or about my beloved Poland, invaded from both sides. Many evenings, we all sat in the lecture hall listening to propaganda speeches that boasted of the virtues and victories of Communism. Maruszka would explain the difficult parts for me, describing how millions of Americans were dying of hunger in the streets, ignored by a heartless capitalist government. Naive as I was, I still understood that we were being fed the Marxist line, and though I didn't believe half of what I heard, my mind was busy, struggling to listen and understand.

But nights were hard. Often, in the adjoining rooms, someone would be having a party, and the smell of cigarettes and the sound of loud laughter and the clinking of glasses would keep me awake, staring at the ceiling, trying not to cry from loneliness and anxiety. *Ojcze nasz, Który jesteś w niebie,* I prayed, *święć się Imię Twoje.* I wondered if the Heavenly Father saw me, alone and defeated. By day I worked in the wards, relearning procedures I had studied in Radom and trying to ignore the fact that I was a prisoner.

'You are making excellent progress,' Dr Pavlovskaya said to me one day

'Thank you, Dr Olga,' I replied. 'Maruszka has been a very good teacher.'

The doctor nodded. She had checked on me frequently, and was always pleased with my work in the hospital and with my efforts to learn Russian. As head of the hospital, her duties were largely administrative, but she kept an eye on me, all the same.

More than Dr Olga, I saw Dr David, a Ukrainian Pole who was head of surgery. He was kind, but demanded the best care for his patients. I was eager to do well for him. It was Dr David who eventually told me where we were: Ternopol, about one hundred kilometres east of Lvov in the Ukraine. I was still in Poland that was not Poland, but I might as well have been in Moscow: I was far, far away from my family, with no way to return to them, or to hear their voices or to see their familiar handwriting on a letter, no way to let them know where I was or even that I was alive.

The weeks went by, and the months, as my Russian improved and my health returned. Dr Olga was transferred to the Finnish front, along with Galla and Maruszka, and was replaced in March by a new administrator, Dr Ksydzof. He was a bitter, sneering man who had suffered some accident in his youth which had left him with a twisted leg that made him limp. Whenever he saw me, he seemed to glare at me with some special hatred. Nothing passed his lips but harsh criticism and complaints about the staff; and soon everyone in the hospital came to despise and fear him.

Under his administration, the Communist propaganda lectures intensified. Almost every night, we were herded into the lecture hall to applaud the latest conquests of the Red Army, which was 'liberating' all of eastern Poland. I had no doubt that all of my compatriots from the forest had been killed, and I began to suspect that Dr Ksydzof intended to bring my stay at the Ternopol hospital to a swift and unpleasant end. Under Dr Olga's authority, I had known I was a prisoner, but I had felt safe. Now, as a nurse of the renegade Polish army, I knew I attracted Dr Ksydzof's personal vengeance.

And yet I did not suspect how it would happen. One night, dead tired from a twenty-four-hour shift, I was awakened by a weight sinking onto my bed beside me, and I was overwhelmed by the stink of stale cigar smoke and vodka. Hands began groping me, and clamped my mouth shut as I began to fight.

'Shut up, you Polish bitch!' a harsh voice growled. 'You're mine now.'

I knew it was Dr Ksydzof. Everything in me recoiled with disgust and horror, and I flailed out, trying to shove him off me. My hand struck the heavy glass bottle of cold tea that I kept on a chair beside the bed, and without thinking, I gripped it by its neck and swung it as hard as I could, smashing it on his head. He went limp, and I struggled out from under him, soaked – with tea, with blood, I wasn't sure.

'*Panie Jezu!* Lord Jesus, I've killed him!' I moaned.

In a panic, I ran from the room in my nightgown, the tiled floor cold on my bare feet. I ran blindly to the emergency room, where I found Dr David sitting alone at the nurses' station, reading a chart.

'Help me! I've killed him! What will happen to me?'

He shoved his chair back and jumped to his feet, gripping my arms. 'Irushka, what is it? Who have you killed?'

I was panting, sobbing, and I shook my head in despair. 'I'll be arrested, they'll execute me! He attacked me while I was sleeping and I killed him!'

Dr David turned away and rummaged in a closet for a

blanket, which he wrapped around me. 'Stay here,' he said, leading me to a bed in a nearby room. He sat me down and tucked the blanket under my knees as I sobbed. 'Try to calm down. We'll figure out what happened.'

When he left I huddled on the bed, rocking myself back and forth, gulping down my tears. He was gone for several minutes, and when he came back, he looked tired.

'Whoever it was is gone – you certainly didn't kill him.'

I stared up at him. 'It was Dr Ksydzof,' I whispered.

Dr David let out a long, slow breath. 'You have an enemy now, for sure. But I don't think he'll bring charges. How would it look for him? He attacked you in your bed.'

He sat beside me, patting my knee. He was kind, and in spite of the way I had been abused by men, I trusted him.

'Let me think about what to do with you,' he continued gently. 'I'd like to get you away from here—'

'Yes! I could go home!'

'No, Irushka. I don't think it's possible to go west yet. But I have some friends . . .'

My disappointment forced fresh tears from my eyes. 'I want to go home,' I said miserably. 'I want my mother.'

'I'm sorry.' Dr David stood up, easing his back. 'Stay here tonight. Tomorrow we'll try to come up with something. I think you're safe from Dr Ksydzof for a while.'

I had little hope of that, but in fact, Dr David was right. No mention was ever made of the incident; it was as though it had never happened. For the next few days, I tried to keep clear of the administrator. But when I did run into him, the looks he gave me squeezed my heart like a fist. He was certainly waiting for an opportunity to punish me, and

I did not know how long I had. Every time I saw Dr David, I wanted to plead with him for news, but there were always other people around, so it was impossible to talk privately.

At last, the chance came. I was able to get away to Dr David's office, and he checked the hallway before closing the door.

'I have a friend, a woman I went to medical school with. She lives in Svetlana, near Kiev. It's a tiny village. She runs the local infirmary; I've told her that you are a good nurse, and what your story is. She'll take you in. But getting you out will be a problem. I can't forge a permit for you.'

'I'll find a way,' I promised. 'I have to get away from here.'

I slipped out of his office and hurried back to my work. Over the next few days, I began studying the hospital grounds for a way out. The gates were guarded by soldiers, and there was no way through them without a permit. But as I strode back and forth across the yard, swinging my arms as though getting exercise, I noticed a loose board in the fence. I bent down to tie my shoe, and studied the board. The opening was narrow, but I was so thin I knew I could squeeze through it. The next time I saw Dr David alone, I told him I had a way out.

'Don't tell me the details. It's better I don't know,' he said quietly. He held up an X-ray in front of us, as though showing it to me. It shielded us from passing eyes. 'I'll get you a train ticket and my friend's address in Svetlana. We have a shift together tomorrow. I'll give it to you then.'

We were both looking at the X-ray, doctor and nurse conferring about a patient. I breathed out slowly, as though I had been holding my breath for days. 'Thank you, Doctor.'

'Good luck, Irushka. Be careful.'

Svetlana Year

It was the middle of March when I left Ternopol. Dirty snow lay in banks on the shady side of the street as I made my way to the train station, early in the morning as the sun rose. Because I had sneaked out after my shift had ended, I knew I would not be missed for several hours. Nobody took any notice of me on the street – I was only one of many hurrying to work or to buy food for the family table. Two Russian soldiers carved themselves thin slices of sausage as they leaned against a boarded-up kiosk in the station; they barely glanced my way when I walked past them and swnng up onto the train. The mighty Red Army was too busy with breakfast to pay attention to me, and I slipped through their net as easily as smoke.

I found a compartment; I travelled east. The train huffed over muddy, half-thawed farmland, rutted deep by wagon wheels. Dark wooden church spires stuck up on the flat horizon, and along the streams stood naked willows. Cinders from the train's smokestack flew backward in a grey cloud. All day long we moved across the countryside, stopping from time to time at a town or village depot. Once, in the distance, I saw an ant line of Red Army trucks crawling westward. I never moved from my seat, but sat with my hands in my lap, keeping small.

At last we crossed the mighty Dnieper River and stopped

for some time at Kiev. The station was a mass of soldiers in Red Army uniforms, but I sat as still as a woodcock in a thorn bush, and no-one saw me in my camouflage. Cars were shunted away; the train jerked as other cars were attached; huge gasps of steam boiled out from under the carriage, and a conductor shouted out the names of the stops on the west-east line.

Then we were gone, and the onion domes and gilded spires of Kiev fell away behind us. A group of soldiers, drunk and noisy, had boarded the train and were stumbling down the passage, looking for pretty girls and singing a dirty song about mules, roughhousing as they came. I pulled my scarf around me and kept my face toward the window. My feet were cold, and my stomach grumbled like an old dog. As darkness began to fall, we slowed for a tiny provincial train station, and a conductor called out, 'Svetlana.'

I fumbled the compartment door open and stepped down onto the platform, almost tripping in my hurry.

'Rachel! It's me, Miriam!'

Strong arms caught me from behind and whirled me around. I stared at a young woman with dark, curling hair peeking out from under a shawl, and she met my gaze. 'It's so good to have you here, *Cousin*,' she said firmly. 'Little Rachel Meyer, how you've grown since I last saw you!'

'Oh, yes,' I stammered.

'Now,' Miriam continued, tucking my arm into hers and shepherding me into the station, 'I know you're tired, so no talk – we'll get home and get you settled. Good night, Comrade,' she said to the man nodding behind the ticket window.

He waved one hand sleepily, not even looking up. 'Good night.'

Then we were on the muddy street, where the twilight was turning everything grey. We walked quickly, not speaking, past two old grey women bundled up in grey scarves, and when we were alone, I got up the courage to speak.

'Dr David said – I thank you so much for taking me in,' I faltered. 'I didn't know what else to do.'

'It's best if you do not speak too much at first,' my new cousin said gently. 'Your accent is a tiny bit off. Let me do the talking for a little while, anyway. We'll have to register you with the district magistrate tomorrow. Remember, you are my cousin, Rachel Meyer from Ludmilla, near Lvov. Tonight you will practise writing your name so that it comes easily to you.'

She unlocked the door of a little house attached to a clinic, and then we were inside in the warmth and light. Miriam unwrapped her scarf and shook her hair out as she looked at me.

'So. You are here. I'll take care of you until we can get you home.'

I walked slowly around the single downstairs room of the cottage. Medical books lay open on a table, and a pot was bubbling on the stove. The house had a cosy, familiar smell of antiseptics, wood smoke, and violet perfume. For the first time in many months, I began to relax. Someone was taking care of me. Those words were a blessing to my poor, lonely heart.

While Miriam and I waited for our dinner to finish cooking, we sat with our feet up on the fender of the stove, toasting our soles and getting acquainted. Then, as we ate dinner – cabbage soup, hot brown bread, fresh milk, and pickled onions – we concocted the details of Rachel Meyer's life, and gradually, the terrible things that had happened to Irena Gutowna began to seem like events in someone else's past. Late that night, there in eastern Ukraine on the broad plain of sleeping wheat fields, I went to sleep as Irena; when I awoke, I was Rachel.

My new life began first thing in the morning, when a young boy was brought into the infirmary with a broken leg. He had fallen while helping to repair the roof of his family's home. Miriam set the bones and I helped her to put a cast on the boy's leg. He was a pale, underfed boy, and he watched us silently. When the father came to carry the boy home, he brought with him a fresh-killed chicken as payment. He laid it on the infirmary table, where it bled on the white enamel.

Over the next several weeks, we were kept busy with the accidents and illnesses of the people of Svetlana. Men got drunk and fought, and we tended them. Women bore children, and we helped their births. The children in the local school needed vaccinations, the old, weathered men and women needed relief from their rheumatism, or needed a tooth pulled or an abscess lanced. We were paid in blood sausages, plucked chickens, creamy milk, dusty bread, honeycombs with dead bees stuck in the wax, labour on demand – everything but money. I kept the medicines in order, I sterilized instruments, I rolled bandages. Miriam was an excellent doctor, and every moment I worked with her I learned something new.

In early May, I was startled to notice lilacs blooming on the roadside as we came home from delivering a baby, and

I realized that my eighteenth birthday was only days away. Then a letter arrived from Dr David, telling of the furore in the Ternopol hospital over my escape. Dr Ksydzof had reported that I was a key member of a dangerous group of subversive Polish partisans, but that shortly after my escape I had been captured and was now rotting away in a Russian jail. Miriam and I chuckled over that, and we were both relieved to know that no suspicion had fallen on Dr David. We were able to celebrate my birthday and my successful escape. We clinked our glasses together, then danced a few steps of a polka while Miriam hummed the tune. On the roof two nest-building storks croaked like gossips.

Svetlana was a tiny village, and I soon knew most of the residents by sight. I was Rachel Meyer, Dr Miriam's little cousin, and they treated me with the same awe and respect they gave her. In the tiny, dirt-floored cottages where we treated colicky babies or bedridden grandmothers, the villagers bowed their heads before us and urged us to sit in their only chairs. They hardly ever spoke to us, except to explain their medical problems. They were poor farmers, mostly, people who had never been outside Svetlana, people who knew nothing of the world beyond their village limits. Communism had changed nothing about peasant life; their lives had been hard before, and they were hard now. A war being fought to the west meant nothing to them.

But I was always conscious of it. When the sun went down every evening, my heart went with it into the west, yearning for my family in Poland. In spite of Miriam's endless kindness and friendship, I missed my home bitterly and never stopped thinking of it. I could not know what was happening in Poland, because I didn't trust the Communist newspapers to report the truth. Some of what they printed was probably correct, but how could I know what was true and what was propaganda?

And so the months went by, and I found myself following country ways: up early in the morning before dawn, hard work all day, hearty simple meals and early to bed. In the summer, there was a typhoid epidemic, and we were busy for six weeks trying to keep death away from our poor people. Fall arrived, when the fields turned to amber and the wheat threshing filled the air with a golden haze. Then winter came down hard, and soon the sound of sleigh bells rang out over the frozen roads. The peasants celebrated Christmas out of sight of the Communist officials. It was now 1941, and I was still in Svetlana. Snow covered the village to the rooftops. Miriam and I stayed inside, warming our feet at the giant wood stove, as usual.

In January, another letter came from Dr David. 'We have learned that the Russians and Germans have agreed to allow Poles who have been separated from their families by the invasion to cross battle lines in the spring. If you know of anyone in that position, you should tell him or her to be ready to come to Ternopol for processing when the time comes.'

'He means me, Miriam,' I whispered. I clutched my hands around a cup to keep them from shaking. 'He means me. I can go home.'

'Yes, but it will be very dangerous for you in Ternopol, Irushka,' she said, folding the letter carefully. 'You may still be wanted by the Red Army. You could be arrested.'

I looked at her, and I guessed that she was frightened for herself and for Dr David. I went to her and knelt by her side. 'Miriam, you must know I would never, ever betray you. But you must let me go. I have to find my family. Please!'

She put one hand on my hair. 'I know, dear. But we must be cautious. We must be very cautious.'

It was nearly impossible for me to contain my excitement, but I also knew I could not simply rush back to Ternopol. We began to study the newspapers every day, waiting for confirmation of Dr David's report. In February, the Communists began to explain, in their usual self-congratulatory way, that the compassionate Soviet Union was allowing Polish families to be reunited. Miriam and I devised a story for the local magistrate to explain my decision to leave. We would say that my mother was dying, that I had to return to Ludmilla to keep house for my father.

Day after day, we waited for final confirmation of the exchange. At last, it was time for me to go. Miriam went with me to the train station early on a cool morning in late March. Our breath fogged in the air. It was almost a year to the day since I had first arrived in Svetlana.

'Be careful what you say,' Miriam warned me as we watched the train chug into the station. 'I wish I could persuade you to stay here, where you are safe, but I know that is impossible. Keep your wits about you at the border. Anything can happen.'

'Oh, I know, I know,' I said quickly, craning my head to watch the train. I turned to her, and suddenly I was crying. 'Miriam, I will miss you so much.'

'Goodbye, my dear cousin,' she replied.

To cover her tears, she reached for a compartment door and hustled me up into the train. 'Goodbye!'

I pressed my face close to the window, not wanting to lose sight of her. As the train moved out, she receded farther and farther into the distance, until she was only a small dark figure by the tracks. Then the rising sun flooded the plain with light, and Miriam disappeared in the glare. I sat back on the wooden bench, and said goodbye to Rachel Meyer as well.

Irena Gutowna was going home again. Home to war.

Through the Gate

· I had to return to Ternopol. There, in the marketplace, would be a registration area for Polish nationals like me who needed to cross into the German sector. The announcement in the newspaper made it sound so simple: I had to be 'processed', and then I would be on my way to rejoin my family. The wheels of the train beat a rhythm as the muddy Ukrainian wheat lands blurred past the windows: *almost home, almost home, almost home*. Crows flapped languidly past my view. The catkins on a stand of birches quivered in a gust of wind. A farmer in a wagon with truck tyres for wheels waited at a crossing, and behind him, the twin-rutted road stretched across undulating plains until the two worn grooves joined in a point.

In wartime, things are slow. The train stopped so many times, there were so many delays and detours to let troop transports by, that it was twenty-four hours before we arrived in Ternopol. I jumped from my seat as the train began slowing and the moment it halted I swung myself down onto the platform. A gust of steam hissed out from under the train, shrouding me for a moment in a cloud. Then the vapour smoked away and I saw the crowds milling around me: families with suitcases, old women with lined faces and sadly tattered city hats, soldiers, police dogs. No young men, of course. I began walking as fast as I could through the crowd.

'The marketplace?' I asked a young woman on the street.

'There, that way,' she said, pointing, and I hurried that way.

I was so close to being reunited with my family! All I had to do was fill out some paperwork, get a transit pass, and be on my way – assuming that nobody recognized me and knew I had escaped a year earlier. My heart filled with excitement as I raced down the stone sidewalk. The street was busy with traffic, the air thick with diesel smoke, and the gutters filled with horse manure. Cigarette smoke hung like a fog at the open door of a café, where old men in dark clothes stood at a bar sipping glasses of tea and reading newspapers printed on thin, flimsy paper. A radio played a scratchy record of patriotic Russian music.

Ahead, I saw a line of people waiting for something, shuffling their feet and speaking tiredly with one another. I began edging past them, giving them scarcely a glance. There was a smell of unwashed bodies, and several babies were crying a monotonous, steady complaint. The line stretched for blocks, and as I made my way along it my steps began to slow. My heart grew heavy again.

'Is this line – is this for the registration to go west?' I asked a man, praying that it was something else, a line for bread, a line for documents, a line for anything but what I wanted.

Even as I spoke, the man nodded and hitched his broken suitcase higher in his arms. 'I have been waiting on this line since yesterday,' he mumbled. 'Those stinking guards – they're taking a long time on purpose, just to spite us.'

He continued grumbling to himself, cursing the Soviets

and the Germans and everyone else. I turned to make my way to the end of the line, but realized that if I was in for such a long wait, I had better find a toilet first. I looked ahead to where the line snaked around a corner, into the marketplace. Perhaps there would be facilities there.

I hugged my coat around my shoulders and continued walking forward, scanning the faces of the refugees as I went. It was foolish of me to think I might recognize someone. But I was so anxious to see my family and loved ones again that I was ready to search for them anywhere, like the drunken man who searches for his money under the streetlight simply because the light is better there. At last, here were my countrymen, and in my ears were Polish voices. Each 'Tatuś or 'Mamusia' I overheard from a child twisted the blade of my homesickness.

I rounded the corner and came into the market square, where the broken pavement glimmered with puddles. Here there was another, shorter line. At the head of this line, above a table, was a sign in both German and Polish: 'Registration for German Citizens and Polish Citizens of German Descent.'

Fear and excitement bolted through me, leaving my fingertips prickling. I was blond and blue-eyed, I spoke German, and I had a German name. I could pass myself off as of German descent. My cheeks flamed with heat as I took my place at the end of the line. I told myself that the ends justified the means. *I* knew I was not German, but *they* would not know I was not German. I had already spent a year lying and deceiving everyone in Svetlana – one more lie meant nothing, and I wanted to go home. I wanted to go home!

In front of me, several people were chatting together, talking conspicuously about their relatives in the Fatherland, dropping names and making admiring comments about Hitler. I thought it was shameful that they would deny their Polishness, but I wondered if they were only acting, playing a part, as I was about to do, if they were doing anything they could just to get home. We must pretend to be German, so we could finally be Polish again.

In less than two hours, I was at the registration table, smoothing back my hair and willing my brain to recall all the German I had learned in high school. A Soviet officer and a German officer sat at the table. I ignored the Russian and addressed the German.

'*Guten Tag, Herr Lieutenant,*' I said, mustering all the poise I could manage.

He glanced at me, taking in my German appearance, and smiled in a fatherly way. '*Guten Tag, Fräulein.* You are alone?'

'Yes,' I continued in German. 'I was separated from my family – they are in Oberschlesien. I am so anxious to return to them.'

'Oberschlesien?' The officer scanned a list on the table. 'Oberschlesien has been repatriated into the Fatherland. Here we can register you for admittance to the Polish General Gouvernement - what's left of Poland. Once there you can see about continuing across the border into Germany.'

Crawling goose bumps prickled along my scalp. Kozłowa Góra had been swallowed into Germany. My voice came out high and false. 'Oh, I see. Will it take very long to register?'

'We will make it as quick as we can. Your name?' he asked.

'Irene Gut.'

Another officer wrote it down; they also took my age, my parents' address, and the reason I had become trapped on the Soviet side. Then the first officer inclined his head.

'Safe journey, Fräulein Gut.'

And with that I was through. I could hardly believe it had been so simple. I walked on, my skin still prickling, expecting at any moment to be called back. But no voice was raised to halt me.

Again I joined the end of a line, this one for transportation processing. The line from the registration of Polish citizens who did not claim any Germanness converged with the line I was in at the building ahead; I decided that I would really rather be with them. After all, I did not know if I would be sent to Germany if I stayed with the German group. I thought it safer to rejoin the line of people expecting to go into German-occupied Poland – the General Gouvernement. What I really wanted to do now was return to Radom and see what my aunt Helen Pawlowska could tell me about the status of things in Kozłowa Góra, in Oberschlesien; if my family was there, I would try to reach them. If not, I would not go to hated Germany. Once I knew where my family was, I could proceed.

That is, assuming I could even find my aunt, and assuming that she knew what had become of my parents and sisters.

Simply strolling across the pavement to the other line and saying, 'Excuse me, may I cut in?' did not seem possible: there were armed guards everywhere keeping an eye on the refugees. We inched closer to the building. A cold, damp breeze blew across the square, blowing grit and scraps of paper into the puddles. Everyone was tired, cold, hungry, and full of restless anxiety. I stood biting my lips and staring at the opposite line.

Suddenly, a woman in the Polish group crumpled in a faint, and the people around her dissolved into a formless crowd. Several women hurried to help her, and I found myself rushing with them. I knelt on the ground beside the fallen woman. My view of the courtyard and the German line was now barred by a forest of legs. I inched backward, deeper into the Polish crowd, and then stood up, wiping my hands on my skirt and leaving my German identity behind. A small girl looked up at me curiously, a strangely adult look in her eyes. I put a finger to my lips and then turned away from her, feeling the pounding beat of my heart grow quieter.

Now there was more waiting, another table, more officers. I bought a transport pass for Radom with the money Miriam had given me. The pass had the time of my train: eight o'clock that evening. I stood looking down at the slip of paper that was my passport back to German-occupied Poland. It fluttered in a breath of wind that blew dust along the pavements, and I clasped it to my heart, suddenly terrified of losing it.

I had no pockets in my dress. I had a little handbag, but I was nervous of pickpockets or thieves. The safest place I could think of to keep my pass was inside my brassiere. Being so thin and small, I had never worn a brassiere before, but Miriam had given me one, telling me to stuff it with cotton to make me look less like the lost and pitiful waif I was. I hurried into the rest room and tucked the precious pass in next to my skin. For extra safety, I cinched my belt tightly around my waist. Now I was ready to go to the train station.

But it was late afternoon, and I had hours to kill before my train left. I wandered the town, gazing idly into shops that had very little to sell, reading the public notices on a signboard. On a bridge over the slender Seret River, I paused to watch the ducks dabbling in the mud. A weak sun came out, striking on the ripples near the bank. I picked at the masonry of the bridge, crumbling the old mortar under my fingers and dropping the pebbles into the water. My stomach grumbled loudly. I headed back into town and found a park, where I sat on a bench in the weak spring sun and tried to teach myself patience. Around me were bare garden beds where bulbs should have been planted, and gravel paths that looked as though they had gone unraked for months. The park had a gloomy, neglected feeling that made me shiver. I was vaguely aware of a loud voice droning nearby in Russian, and I cupped my ear to hear the words.

'How lucky we are that Mother Russia saved us from the capitalists! Now everyone is the same, from the president down to the lowliest worker!'

It was the usual Communist propaganda, but I was curious to see who was delivering this monotonous lecture in the middle of an empty park. I was about to rise from my seat to follow the voice, when I saw two Russian soldiers walking toward me along the path. Their boots crunched loudly on the gravel.

They stared at me as they passed, and I blushed and

ducked my head, not wanting them to try to flirt with me. They walked on by. I let out a small sigh of relief, but even as I did I felt a strange prickle of worry. Something about them seemed slightly familiar. There was only one place I could have met them before: the Ternopol hospital. I jumped up from the bench and began walking as quickly as I could.

I was seriously alarmed. Had they recognized me? I cursed myself for being so careless. Why had I dawdled all over Ternopol, showing myself to the whole town? Had I lost my senses? I had more than my own safety at stake: I had promised Dr David and Miriam I would not endanger them. The voice I had followed was very loud now, although I saw no-one. At last, I realized the voice was coming from a loud-speaker attached to a statue of Lenin. 'How lucky we are!' it began again in the same dreary tone. On the statue's shoulders hunched two pigeons who tipped their heads and fixed me with their black eyes.

It was as though the statue were watching me, lecturing me, mocking me for thinking I could get home. I shuddered violently and looked back over my shoulder to see if the two soldiers were following me. I clutched at my chest, feeling the dry whisper of paper against my skin. I had only a few hours to wait for my train. I would hide at the train station, among the crowds. I would keep to myself and try to remember that I had other people's secrets to keep safe.

I heard footsteps behind me, and across a stretch of muddy lawn I saw a Russian patrol walking toward the bench I had just vacated. My stomach rolled over. Slowly, not wanting to attract any attention, I began walking toward the park gate. Like an ostrich, I kept my head down, praying not to be seen.

And then into my field of view, hard and black against the gray gravel, came army boots. I stopped, and looked up into the faces of another Russian patrol.

The loudspeaker behind me continued to drone, 'How lucky we are that Mother Russia has saved us!'

'This way,' they said, taking my arms and leading me between them through the gate.

My Heart, Like a
Netted Bird

At the commissariat I was put in a small, windowless room. The only furnishings were a table and a chair, and a single lightbulb in the ceiling – the usual stereotyped shabby furniture you see in any movie with an interrogation scene, I noticed. I was able to view my surroundings with this kind of detachment, in spite of being terrified. There was just some part of me that could not believe it was real, that I could not possibly be in this scene.

My fear made it all too real, very quickly. I sat pressing my knees together to keep them from trembling. *'Ojcze nasz, Który jesteś w niebie, święć się Imię Twoje . . .'* Over and over I whispered the words of the Modlitwa Pańska, the Our Father. I counted Hail Marys on my fingers, but each time I heard a voice in the corridor, or a strange noise from somewhere else in the building, I froze and lost my place in my prayers. Hours went by, I think. I do not know for sure.

At last the door opened, and two guards told me to follow them. I dared not look right or left as we walked to the commissar's office. I did not know what terrible things might be happening behind closed doors, or what might be in store for me. My detachment came and went in waves: one moment I was an observer of the scene, the next moment I was afraid I might wet myself from fear.

I stepped into the office, and saw, to one side, the two soldiers I had recognized in the park. My little handbag was on the commissar's desk. A picture of Stalin occupied the wall behind the desk.

'That is the spy Irena, who worked in the hospital,' one of the soldiers said the moment I entered.

The commissar, who looked disturbingly like Stalin himself, dismissed them. They saluted and left. I stood with my arms pressed tight against my ribs. Violent tremors went through me, as though I were freezing to death.

'Take off your jacket,' the commissar ordered.

I willed my fingers not to tremble as I unbuttoned my jacket. I handed it to one of the guards, and he searched it thoroughly. I heard stitches rip as he shoved his large hand into one of the pockets.

'Empty your other pockets,' the commissar said in a deep, expressionless voice.

'I don't have any other pockets,' I quavered.

'Where is your gun?'

I almost laughed at the absurdity, but I was too frightened. 'I don't have a gun. I have never had a gun. What would I do with a gun?'

The commissar looked at one of the guards and jerked his chin. The man immediately began frisking me. My face flooded with shame as he ran his hands over me. Still tucked into my brassiere was my transit pass, but by now my train must have gone without me.

'Now you will answer some questions.'

'But I don't know any—'

'Sit down.'

The desk lamp was turned toward me, shining into my face and turning the rest of the room dark.

They asked me my name, where I was from, why I had been in Ternopol, how I had ended up in the hospital. I stumbled through my answers like a bad liar, but I swore repeatedly that I was telling the truth – and I *was* telling the truth.

'With what organization are you connected now? It will go easier for you if you tell us the truth. What are the partisans planning?' The deep voice rumbled at me from behind the light.

'I am alone — all alone,' I said. My stomach was jerking and quivering. 'I don't know anything.'

He repeated his questions as one of the soldiers laboriously wrote down everything I said. I pressed one hand to my chin to keep it from shaking. The same questions: where were the partisans? Who was in charge? What were they planning? I began to cry, knowing they did not believe me and unable to convince them of my innocence. The commissar was fixated on the story Dr Ksydzof had spread. He was convinced that I had been planted at the hospital on purpose, as though my rape had been part of an elaborate scheme. 'They raped me,' I sobbed. 'Your soldiers. They raped me and beat me.'

At last the commissar planted his hands on his desk and pushed his chair back. The edges of the light caught the whiskers of his thick moustache. 'Take her away,' he said. 'We will try again later.'

A different cell. A cot and a blanket. I curled up in a ball, and fragments of prayers darted through my mind as I fell in and out of sleep. Then I was dragged awake and back to the commissar's office, where we went through the questions again. Where were the partisans, what were they planning? There were threats of prison in Siberia, threats of torture. I felt as though I had become nothing but a tiny voice whispering to the glare of the light. They were convinced that I was hiding something, and I was: I never mentioned Dr David or Miriam. But my face must have proved me a liar: they hounded me for hours. Obviously they did not believe my story, and even to myself it began to sound untrue. To explain my year-long absence I said I had gone from village to village, working for food, sleeping in barns, hiding out. But my story was so flimsy they knew it was a lie. Again I was taken to the cell where I fell into some nightmare sham of sleep, and again I was shaken awake and interrogated.

By morning I was exhausted. When the guards took me to the commissar's office, I found him eating a plate of eggs and sausage. He stabbed at his eggs, making the yolks run. I watched him with a kind of disbelief. It seemed like ages since I had last eaten.

'Do you wish to repeat your story, or is there anything you would like to add?' he asked through a mouthful. Drops of golden yolk dotted his moustache. I felt sick to my stomach, watching him and smelling the food, but I could not take my eyes off his plate. There was a red and polished apple beside it.

'Do you wish to add anything to your story?' he said again, spearing a sausage with his knife.

'I ran away from the hospital when Dr Ksydzof tried to

rape me,' I said, swallowing hard. 'I have told you this and I know you don't believe me, but it is the truth.'

He put his knife and fork down, and riffled through some papers, which he flapped at me. 'We have a different story from the doctor. Whom do you expect me to believe?'

'Dr Ksydzof,' I whispered.

He grunted, and then gestured with his fork; the guard took me back to my cell. It was impossible for me to tell how much time had gone by, how long I had been there, or even what time of day it was. The commissar had been eating breakfast, but I had begun to doubt the reality of everything around me. Just because he was eating eggs and sausage did not mean it was morning, and even if it was, I did not know which morning. At some point, I was brought cold tea and some bread, which I wolfed down and which immediately made me feel like vomiting. I held my hand over my mouth and squeezed my eyes shut, willing myself not to be sick. I swallowed and swallowed the flood of saliva that filled my mouth.

Once again, I was led to the commissar's office. This time, I sensed something had changed. He waved me to a chair and placed a glass of hot tea in front of me. I picked it up and cupped my hands around it, watching him nervously as I sipped.

To my surprise, the man smiled. 'You know, I have decided I believe you,' he began. He folded his arms on the desk and leaned toward me. 'You are young and pretty – so helpless. I would like to help you.'

The tea stuck in my throat. I did not believe a word he was saying. I did not trust his new manner any more than the old one.

'You must have some friends nearby who can help you. When you escaped from the hospital you must have stayed with someone . . .' His voice trailed off in a question.

I blew on my tea, stalling. I did not know what to say. My mind was sluggish and words took a long time to sink in.

'There must be someone you can stay with while we sort this all out,' the commissar continued. 'Dr Ksydzof is in Moscow, but he will be back soon and we can finally put all the pieces together. In the meantime, you may go stay with your friends and get some rest. I know our accommodations haven't been very . . . very comfortable for a young lady.'

I blew on my tea again. 'I know a girl,' I said slowly. The words came like lines I had memorized. I did not know where they came from. 'Her name is Lalka.'

'Yes?' he said, leaning forward again. 'You would like to stay with her tonight?'

Through my mind ran a memory of my dog Lalka chasing a stick into a stream, the water splashing up around her and sparkling in the sun. 'Very much,' I said fervently.

He smiled, and then sat back and uncapped a pen. 'Tell me her last name and her address, and we can take you to her home.'

I glanced up at the picture of Stalin over the desk. I felt as though I were in a play, or as if I were speaking someone else's part. 'I don't remember her last name, Commissar; I don't know her that well. And I don't know the name of the street, either,' I hurried on as he began to frown. 'You know how it is - you know how to get there, even if you don't know what the streets are called.'

His friendly attitude completely changed. He had expected to follow the little thread of Irena Gutowna to the whole ball of partisan yarn. Now he was back in the tangle. 'Do you think I am an idiot?' he barked.

Tears, true tears, began sliding down my cheeks. 'I am sorry – I am so mixed up and tired, I don't remember the name of the street. But I can find my way.'

He sat glaring at me for several moments. Tears ran down my face faster than I could wipe them away. At last he strode from behind his desk and opened the door, calling a guard.

'You will go with Miss Gutowna. She knows the way. And you,' he added, rounding on me suddenly, 'you will be back here at eight in the morning.'

'Oh, yes,' I promised. I would have promised anything to get out of there.

I walked out of his office, and he followed me to the door, watching me as I walked down the corridor with the guard. We walked past the cell I had spent such hateful hours in, and then went through a security gate and to the outer door.

A bright moon lit the street. Not a soul was in sight. Hardly any lights showed at windows. It was after curfew, and Ternopol was a dead city without a single mourner.

'I – I think it is this way,' I stammered to my guard as I turned left.

Our footsteps echoed off the buildings, and our shadows walked ahead of us. I turned down one street, and then another, trying to think what to do. I was cold, and I shoved my hands into my jacket pockets.

'You're sure you know where you're going?' the

guard asked as we passed a synagogue.

'Yes – you see, I have to go the way I am familiar with, and I am sorry it takes so long but – ah, here it is!'

Ahead of us, a three-storey building reared up into the darkness. Beside it was a fence with a board missing. The guard looked up at the building, noting the number above the door.

'Thank you,' I said quickly. 'Thank you. This is it. My friend lives here. I will be back tomorrow.'

I put my hand on the doorknob, and he gave me a quick look before turning and walking away.

'Idiot,' I said under my breath. The moment he turned the corner, I slipped out of the doorway and through the gap I had spotted in the fence. I ran across the dark yard, barking my shin on a metal watering can that toppled, clanking like a broken bell. Then I scrambled over another fence, and across another yard, and I was running as fast as I could down an alley. A back door opened. An old man stepped out, heading for an outhouse.

'Train station?' I asked.

He jumped, startled, as I stepped out of the shadows. Without a word, he pointed down the alley with a knobby finger, and I sprinted away again. When I burst out onto the street, I slowed my pace and kept to the shadows, afraid of attracting attention on the deserted curfew streets. Then, with a gasp of relief, I recognized the bulky silhouette of a church near the station. Moments later, I was in the waiting room.

People were sleeping everywhere – on benches, out on the platform, huddled among their belongings. Boxes and bundles tied with twine served as pillows, and coats were tucked up to chins like blankets. At the far end of the platform, two German guards stood smoking. My hand shook as I reached into my dress and felt for my transit pass. I tried to compose myself as I walked toward them. I had no idea what I looked like after the days of interrogation.

'Sir, can you help me?' I asked, holding out my pass. 'I was sick with a cold and missed my transport on Friday. What can I do?'

Both of the guards examined my paper, and one of them blew smoke out of the side of his mouth. 'You are in luck, Fräulein. The trains have been delayed for two days. Yours has not departed yet. It leaves at five in the morning.'

The hairs on my arms stood up. 'I can leave on the next train? I can go home?'

'Go home, go to Kraków and dance with the Gypsies in the marketplace, whatever you want, little girl.'

They laughed, eyeing me with careless amusement. The one with my pass held it out, then snatched it away with another laugh. My heart thrashed like a netted bird.

'Here you go,' he said, handing it over for real.

I crumpled it in my fist. I would not let it go again until it got me onto the train. I was almost home: I would let nothing stop me from leaving the hated Soviets and their Red Army soldiers and returning to Radom the next day

And yet I did not count on the Germans. On the train, we pressed our faces to the grimy windows as we steamed westward, and voices rose with breathless laughter. But as we crossed the border that separated Soviet-held territory from the German-controlled General Gouvernement of Poland, our train came to a halt and we were ordered off at gunpoint. Many of us were too astonished and frightened to protest, and as we stumbled, blinking, into the sunlight, we saw a barbed-wire fence stretching away on either side. Many women screamed, and children wailed with fear.

'It's a quarantine, you ignorant fools!' a guard said, sneering. 'We can't have you spreading filthy Russian diseases. Get in there.'

I felt my stomach quivering as I shuffled forward in a group with the other refugees. We had no idea what to expect: the indignities of quarantine camp took my breath away – inspection, disinfection, segregation, humiliation.

Within hours of our arrival at camp, rumours began to circulate – slowly at first, and then faster. The men, who had been separated from the women upon arrival, were being examined for circumcision; the circumcised men, the Jews, were taken away. To where? Why? Would they be back? No one knew. Daily, we were forced to assemble in the muddy yard and listen to threats and warnings from the commandant. Enemies of the Third Reich would be punished. Walking near the fence and guard towers was forbidden. We were required to work for our 'room and board', our hard-bunk barracks and our unadorned potatoes. Hitler's welcome-home message to us was loud and clear: obey, or suffer.

One day, my resistance to camp life worn down, I could not rise from my bunk to report for my duties in the kitchen. Within moments, the guards came to roust me. '*Aufstehen!*' a soldier shouted.

He ripped the thin blanket off me, and I cried out weakly in German: '*Nein! Ich bin krank!*' No, I am sick!

The guard froze, and then took a closer look at me.

'*Warten Sie, Fräulein.* Wait here. I did not know you are German. I'll get the doctor.'

The infirmary was a marginal improvement. I was suffering from influenza, which had broken out in the unsanitary, crowded conditions of the camp: so much for German efficiency in a quarantine camp. We in the infirmary learned not to be too fussy as patients, because it was obvious that the German medical staff had little tolerance for the Poles. We tried to lie low and get better fast. April came and was nearly gone before I was able to leave my sickbed. I was weak; all my senses were ratcheted up. The gentlest touch made me wince. Lights seemed brighter to me, and even soft noises startled me.

At last, I was given new documents and a pass for the train. This time, when I boarded, I pleaded with God and the Virgin to let nothing else prevent me from reaching Radom. Our transport was a cattle car, and we stood pressing our faces to the slits between the boards as we headed west once again. Fresh green spring air blew through the cars as we sped across the Polish countryside. Along a fence line I saw purple lilacs bowing in the breeze, and I didn't know if I wanted to laugh or cry. Since becoming sick I'd cried easily. Now tears flowed as I watched my homeland flash by between the planks.

When I finally set foot in Radom again after my two years in exile, I found the city had changed. For one thing, many familiar landmarks had been destroyed in the bombing: the shells of apartment buildings and schools stood crumbling into ruin, and piles of broken masonry towered in empty lots. Only the factories seemed to be working, their stacks oozing black smoke. Also, all the streets had been given German names, and I had to find my way around by memory. I walked slowly, trailing my fingers along the faces of buildings like a blind woman. Turn left at this ruined heap – of the Wawel Hotel, was it? – and down a street now called Hermann Göring Strasse. I turned and turned, growing more bewildered all the time. The Germans had bestowed new names on the city, but had spent nothing to repair the damage they had inflicted.

'You look lost, young lady. Can I give you a ride somewhere?'

I turned to see a man with bushy grey eyebrows regarding me from a buggy. His two horses swished their tails and rubbed their fetlocks with their noses.

'I have no money to pay you, sir,' I replied.

'They can't all be paying customers.' He patted the seat beside him. 'Come on. Up you go. Where are you trying to go?'

I was still looking this way and that, trying to get my bearings. 'I don't know the new name of the street my aunt lives on . . .'

'Tell me the old name. I've lived here all my life. You can't make this town German just like that.' With that he snapped the reins and the horses clip-clopped into action. He kept up a steady chatter as we drove, bragging about his pretty daughter, Zofia, and his son, Tadeusz. As things began to look familiar to me, I started trembling with nervousness.

'I recognize that church,' I said, grabbing his arm. 'My aunt's house is very close! Oh, what if she's not there? I'll have to go to Germany alone to find my parents, and—'

'One thing at a time. One thing at a time.'

The old buggy jounced and jiggled down the street, around craters still unfilled since the blitz – and my aunt Helen's house came into view. Standing at the gate was a girl with black, curly hair. She took one look at me and ran shrieking to the house.

'Irena! Irena!' she screamed. 'It's Irena!' The door burst open at her touch and she fled inside, still screeching.

All the hairs on my body stood up as though I had touched an electric wire. 'Bronia!' I whispered. 'She is little Bronia!'

Tears flooded my eyes. I fell more than climbed down from the buggy. Distantly, I heard its wheels whirring away as I fumbled for the gate. In my haste and excitement, I could not work the catch. I heard a cry from the house, and when I looked up, Mamusia and Tatuś were framed in the doorway.

Like a bird freed from a net, my heart flew up to the sky.

part two

Finding Wings

When I Thought I
Could Be Happy

Tell me the happiest you have ever been, and I can say that on that day, I was happier. Our tears wet each other's cheeks as I kissed my parents and my sisters Marysia and Bronia and Władzia. 'Janina?' I asked, holding my father's hand to my face. 'Where is Janina?'

'She has a job in a restaurant,' Mamusia said as she stroked my hair. 'She'll be home soon.'

We cried and hugged each other, and I laughed and ruffled little Władzia's curls, and I did not have a handkerchief but sniffled and had to wipe my nose with the back of my hand, and then we all began crying afresh as we moved in an awkward clump of embracing bodies into the house.

Bit by bit, I began to take in my surroundings. I had interrupted some task on the dining room table, where there were scraps of rubber tyres and piles of blankets. A large cone of coarse black thread stood amid the jumble.

'We make carpet slippers,' Tatuś explained, flushing slightly. His chin jutted, and I saw that the collar of his shirt gaped around his neck. He had lost so much weight. 'It earns us some money.'

Mamusia picked up a pair of heavy scissors and began

cutting a blanket. 'Enough to help out poor Helen. Her husband was killed in the first fighting.'

With a sister holding each of my hands, I pushed a chair to the table and watched my family work. As they pieced together cheap slippers from retreads and mothy fabric, we took turns piecing together our stories. I had been gone from Radom for twenty months, but I had been separated from my parents and sisters even longer – nearly two years. We had lost precious time as a family.

And the war had taken its toll on them. Tatuś had lost his job: all Polish intellectuals and professionals had been ousted by the invading Germans. Most had been sent to prison camps; many had been executed – at least, that was what everyone assumed. Men had disappeared and never been heard from again. That made poor Tatuś, reduced to sewing black-market slippers, one of the lucky ones. Mamusia's dark hair had turned completely grey since I last saw her. Kozłowa Góra and the rest of Oberschlesien had been snapped up by Germany, and my family, along with many others, had fled eastward, into the 'independent' Poland now known as the General Gouvernement. It was as independent as a prisoner in leg irons.

'Now we live like slaves, or worse,' Tatuś said, frowning, as he used an awl to punch a hole in a rubber sole. 'All Poles are subject to the death penalty for violating curfew or selling black-market goods, or for demonstrating a "hostile mentality"—'

'What could be more subjective?' Mamusia broke in.

'We must step off the sidewalk and remove our hats if a German approaches,' Tatuś continued, still drilling with great concentration. 'And the death penalty is automatic for anyone helping the Jews.'

I felt a chill drive away our joy. 'Helping the Jews?' I asked, squeezing Bronia's hand. 'Helping the Jews do what?'

Mamusia and Tatuś exchanged a glance. 'Live. Work. Get away,' Mamusia said. 'They are – they are not wanted by the Germans.'

I was baffled. 'Then why don't the Germans let them leave?'

'I don't think that is what Hitler has in mind,' Tatuś began carefully. 'I am afraid—'

We heard the door open, and a cheery voice that brought fresh tears of joy to my eyes sang out, 'I'm home! Where is everyone?'

Janina walked into the dining room, shaking her hair as she pulled off her hat. She froze when she saw me.

'Irena!'

We both screamed at the same time and ran into each other's arms. 'I can't believe it!' she cried, jumping up and down with me. 'I can't believe you're real!' We found Bronia and Władzia and Marysia in the embrace with us, and all five of us laughed and sobbed as we clung together, together again.

That night, when we sat down to dinner with Aunt Helen, Tatuś spoke a special prayer of thanksgiving for our safe reunion. In that time of war, it was almost a miracle that our family was intact. Our home, our beautiful villa in Kozłowa Góra, was gone; all our possessions, our mementoes, our photographs and books – everything was gone. But we were together. We were lucky.

That night, after the younger girls were in bed, I told my parents the full story of what had happened to me since the invasion in 1939. Janina held my hand as I faltered through the story of my desperate days in the forest with the Polish army, and my voice sank to a whisper when I told my loved ones that I had been raped. There, safe with my family, I began to weep anew at what the soldiers had done to me.

Tatuś leaned across the table and put his hand on my shoulder. 'Irenka, my dear girl. War makes men animals. You must not let this ruin your life. God has plans for you. He did not let you die. God has plans for you.'

I caught his hand and kissed it, while the hot tears squeezed out between my lashes. 'Yes, Tatuś. I must believe that. But it is very hard.'

The next day, Janina took me on a tour of Radom, now so different from what I remembered that it was like a new city, where even the street names glorified the Third Reich. The restaurant where she worked was run by a Polish couple, but it served only Germans: the Poles could not afford restaurants anymore. Everywhere we went, there were German soldiers and officers of the Wehrmacht, and SS men in black uniforms. Savage-looking Alsatian dogs strained at their leashes, egged on to viciousness by their handlers. We saw swastika-studded signs posted at frequent intervals along the streets, listing the rules by which the Poles must now live. There were many rules. The punishments for breaking them were strict.

And pasted on the walls were posters – cruel, mocking posters – caricaturing the Jews, who were linked to every depravity and sin. Every woe and affliction of the Polish people was laid at their feet. Loudspeakers on street corners blared warnings about the Jews in Polish and German. As we passed the mouth of an alleyway, I noticed three Nazis shouting at an old Jewish man crouched at their feet; he was trying to pluck his yarmulke from beneath one Nazi's boot. Janina took my arm and hustled me down the sidewalk, her face pale. I could not believe my senses, but every time I tried to ask Janina what it was all about, she shook her head and glanced from side to side, on the lookout for Germans.

'This is Poland, now,' Janina said from the side of her mouth.

Without more words, she led me down Reichstrasse. I stared in disbelief at everything I saw, and stumbled when Janina pulled me off the sidewalk to let Germans pass. 'Where are we going?' I muttered, keeping my head down.

'I want you to see something.'

We headed south to Glinice, a Jewish section of Radom. As we approached the district, I saw newly built fences topped with barbed wire stretching across streets. I did not want to ask what the fences meant.

At last we paused, and Janina pretended to be fixing my collar. She turned me to face across the street. There was a gate, guarded by German soldiers and dogs. A large sign warned against typhus. The word *Verboten* screamed at me from across two lanes of traffic.

'Glinice ghetto,' Janina murmured, patting my collar into place. 'All the Jews from Radom and the surrounding countryside have been forced to move in there, and into Walowa ghetto.'

Then, in a bright, false voice, she said, 'Let's go home,

Irenka!' She gave a dazzling smile to a couple of soldiers as we hurried by.

'But what does it mean?' I asked under my breath.

'We don't know.'

Thus was my reunion with my family cast into shadow. We did not know what was going on. Rumours passed with each exchange of ration coupons for bread or cheese. Some said that Hitler was planning to exterminate the Jews, but in our family, we thought that was simply too preposterous to believe. Many of our neighbours in Radom figured the condition of the Jews was the Jews' problem: we Poles had enough of our own, with the brutal way we were being treated.

My nineteenth birthday was marked with only a small celebration. A few days later, I reported to the *Arbeitsamt* to register for work; I was issued an *Arbeitskarte* and a *Kennkarte*, my working papers and identity card. Because of my fluency in German, I was assigned to a German-run restaurant, but the place was hateful to me, filled with smoke and half-drunk soldiers trying to feel me up as I passed with heavy trays. Even the owner cornered me in the pantry one day; he was begging for a kiss when his wife caught him. I was fired. Shortly thereafter I found another job, in a small Polish-run shop near Aunt Helen's home, and that seemed ideal. It was close to home, and I was not surrounded all day by Germans.

So we passed through May and into June, and although food was scarce and we were all working hard just to get by, we took joy every day in knowing that our family was together. We were crowded in Aunt Helen's little house, but we consoled ourselves with songs, just as we had in the old days. When we gathered around the table, raising our voices and laughing over forgotten lyrics, we could almost imagine nothing was wrong. If we could just hold out until the end of the war, we believed, things must surely get better.

But June brought news that Germany and the Soviet Union were now fighting each other; the wary peace between them had fallen apart. Janina and I lay awake at night, listening to our parents whisper in the next bed about how much longer now the war would last. When we eavesdropped on our parents this way, neither Janina nor I acknowledged to the other that we were awake. I think, for each other's sake, we wanted to pretend that we did not know how worried our parents were. But the moonlight would catch a corner of Janina's eye, glinting as she stared at the ceiling; sometimes a tear shone like oil. She was seventeen, and she had grown up fast in the last two years, but I felt a hundred years older. I felt that I had suffered my allotment of pain during my exile, and like a selfish child I wanted my life to be good and happy again. I thought I should be allowed to be happy once more.

But even as I made the wish, it was destroyed: the Germans came one day in July and took Tatuś away.

We were stunned. We sat at the dining room table like victims of a fire, red-eyed and speechless. The ceramics factory Tatuś had designed in Kozłowa Góra was important to the war effort, and the Reich needed his expertise to help make it function. The Germans wanted him; they took him.

For several weeks we heard nothing; then a letter from Tatuś came, and Mamusia broke down weeping over his news: strangers in our house, old friends turning away from Tatuś because he was working for the Germans. When she was recovered enough to speak, she announced that she would take the three younger girls and go to Tatuś in Kozłowa Góra. However, she had heard rumours that young Polish women with Germanic features were being put into brothels in Germany; she would not risk taking me and Janina to Oberschlesien.

To me and Janina, it was as though we had woken from one nightmare into another. First Tatuś was gone. Now Mamusia, Marysia, Bronia, and Władzia were leaving us all at once. I could not believe this was happening so soon after I'd been reunited with my family. They were vanishing before my very eyes, like thistledown in the wind. Janina and I begged Mamusia to take us with her, but she was adamant. We pleaded with her, sobbing, all the way to the train station. We made ourselves sick with weeping, and gagged on our own tears. But when the train left, our mother and sisters were on it and we had been left behind.

Now that they were gone, Janina and I grew even closer, desperate to stay together. Leaving for work every day broke our hearts, for each parting was a reminder of the people we loved who had left. The house was emptier now, but we continued to share a bed, where we held hands each night until we fell asleep. I felt responsible for Janina; I felt I must protect her from the evil that was abroad in our world.

Life in Radom grew harsher. The Polish people were not submitting to the occupation like sheep. There were acts of sabotage against the Germans all the time, but these rebellions were met with reprisals as swift, arbitrary, and deadly as lightning. Men were grabbed from the streets, thrown against walls, and shot. Six men at a time. Ten men. It did not matter to the Germans if those men were responsible for the sabotage, or how many Poles they killed – on the contrary, the more the better. Rapid gunfire was the metronome that kept time in our lives. We learned not to look when we heard the rattle of machine guns or the dull tock-tock of a Luger.

And to support the fighting against the British in North Africa, and against the Russians on the eastern front, the Germans were determined to make Poland work, work hard. Every day, we heard of another friend or neighbour caught in a roundup, a *łapanka*. The leaders of the General Gouvernement were combing the population for workers, men and women between eighteen and forty, and trucking them away.

Where did they go? No one knew, but everyone had a guess. To Germany? To the eastern front? Some people said the prisoners were taken for slave labour. Others worried that the Germans needed conscripts to fight the Allies and the Russians. The gloomiest speculated that the Poles were simply being put into prisons, or killed outright. The Germans despised us, and we knew it. They made it obvious with every crushing rule, with every public de-nunciation, every arbitrary punishment. They scourged us. Night and day, heavy transport trucks whined and growled through the city. The sound would halt us in our work, make us pause with a spoon halfway to our lips, wonder-ing who was on that truck. And make us bear the dread until we saw our loved ones again.

And even as the Poles were being shipped away, Jews were arriving. Sometimes, on my way to buy food, or to follow up a rumour of toilet paper or lightbulbs or real leather shoes, I would see a line of them being marched to the Walowa or Glinice ghetto. Some were well dressed in expensive city clothes in the latest styles and carried bulging suitcases; others looked less prosperous and carried their few worldly goods in cord-wrapped blankets; but all of them looked frightened. I did not see how so many people could keep squeezing into the ghettos; I could not even guess what the conditions were like there.

Late summer and early fall had once been a time of mushroom hunting and hayrides for me. In 1941 those were months of work and fear. We did not hear from Mamusia and Tatuś. We could only pray that our family was safe in Kozlowa Góra, thinking of us as much as we thought of them.

Most of our free time was spent devising ways to get more food, because we were always hungry. The policy of the General Gouvernement allowed very little food for Poles – less than half that allotted to Germans. We dutifully traded in our ration coupons, and what we got in return seemed no more substantial than the paper coupons themselves. It was obvious to me that I was anaemic; the symptoms were familiar from my outlaw days in the eastern forests. Janina was sometimes able to bring left-overs home from the restaurant where she worked, but they were not enough to keep three adults healthy. Aunt Helen, Janina and I were thin and pale, like all the other non-German residents of Radom.

One Sunday, when I was not too tired, I took myself to church, looking for some comfort. I stood, and kneeled, and sat, and mumbled my responses by rote, but the mass did not give me the solace I craved. My mind wandered, fretting over my constant worries. How would we heat the house come winter? Where could I get Janina a warm coat? Who might be baking bread without too much sawdust in it? When would we hear from Tatuś and Mamusia?

As the priest began intoning a benediction, I noticed a bird, a pigeon, fluttering up in the nave. I followed it with my eyes as it tried first one round window and then another, and its frantic beats sent a rain of dust slanting down through the light. It banged against a window, stuttering with its wings. I felt the urge to cry out, to beg someone to help the bird escape, and then a confusion of sound came from outside the church. Motors raced and doors slammed, and there was a pounding of boots on the steps. There were indistinct shouts of command beyond the vestibule. In the congregation, people began turning in the pews and whispering, their eyes wide with fear. Several people got up and began edging along the aisle toward the sacristy, and one old woman began rocking back and forth, clutching her rosary and whispering her prayers through trembling lips. The priest faltered in his blessing, and his voice trailed off.

Everyone was uncertain what to do. Were the soldiers looking for someone in particular? Was it a łapanka? Obviously, we could not stay in the church all day, but people were clearly frightened of going out. I could not take my eyes off the pigeon, still banging at the high windows. I had the wild thought that if the bird could only escape, everything would be all right. Someone jostled me, climbing past me to get to the aisle. At last, two greybeards strode to open the sanctuary doors. The look on their faces should have thrown the desecrators into hell.

But it didn't. The uniformed soldiers were a dark mass against the brightness of the Sunday morning outside. With shouts of *'Raus! Zum Strasse!'* they herded us into the square in front of the church, which was ringed with more Wehrmacht soldiers pointing their guns. The priest tried pleading with an officer, but he was brushed aside.

A wail went up from the parishioners as the soldiers strode into the crowd and began pulling people aside. A young woman shrieked as she was parted from her old mother; two young boys cried as their father was yanked away. To one side, a crowd of children and the elderly. To the other side, youths and the middle-aged.

'Please get word to my sister and my aunt,' I whispered to the priest. 'Helena Pawlowska and Janina Gutowna. Tell them what happened.'

'Stille!' A soldier lunged toward me, but I ducked away and went quickly where I was supposed to go. I felt the muscles in my back clench and twitch as I walked past a row of machine guns to the group of fit workers.

'Where will they take us?' a red-haired woman groaned, clutching her husband's arm.

'I don't know,' he replied. He was trying to be brave for her, I could see.

Three troop transport vehicles roared into the church square, and we were chased into them. Some people cried, others cursed as we were driven to a camp snarled with barbed wire.

'You will be transported to Germany to work for the Reich,' an officer informed us as we stood before our new barracks. 'You Poles have been idle long enough.'

A tangible flood of grief swamped us where we stood. Several women began weeping anew. I felt again the strange detachment, the disbelief that this was happening to me. I stared at my hands as though they were the hands of a stranger.

A dignified, middle-aged man stepped forward to address the officer. 'I must protest. You have no right to treat us in this manner,' he said. 'We must be allowed to contact our families.'

Without a word, two guards stepped forward and clubbed the man to the ground with their rifle butts. We stood watching, horrified and sick at heart, hearing the sound of the blows. Blood was trickling from the man's ears by the time the soldiers were finished. He lay splayed in the dirt, his shoes beaten off him and his arms curled around his head, and not one of us dared go to him.

'I think we understand each other now,' the officer said.

At last, when the officer left us, two men hurried forward to help the beaten man. The October sun was still strong, and in the heat the smell of blood and urine that came from the man on the ground reminded me of a hospital ward. I waved away a fly and went to see how I could help.

We were hauling the man to his feet when another truck roared into the camp and came to a stop. A cloud of dust settled around it as a Nazi major climbed down from the passenger side and tugged his hat to set it more securely on his head. He was an older man, closer to seventy than sixty, and he breathed through his mouth as though he had a stuffed nose.

'You and you,' he said, pointing to one man and then another. 'And you.'

One by one, he picked out ten men and women, almost at random. Last, he pointed to me.

'Into the truck.'

Without further ado, he climbed back in and slammed the door. Newly alarmed, we ten hurried toward the back of the troop transport. A soldier let down the tailgate and hustled us in with the point of his gun.

'Now what?' one woman asked.

'*Matka Boska*,' a man swore softly.

'Please, God, let Janina know I am all right,' I whispered. 'Please look after her for me.'

The driver gunned the engine, and the truck jerked forward, rocking us against one another. We had no way to know where they were taking us. I craned my head to see out the back, for what I feared was my last view of Poland.

Major Rügemer

It must be said that I was now a slave. What else do you call someone put to work in an ammunition factory, kept under guard, and paid no wages? My one comfort was that – despite all my fears – I was still in Poland. Still in Radom, even. The transport truck had brought us back to town, and we were put into barracks. I did not recognize the part of town we were in, and I could not tell how far from home I was. I did not know how to get word to Janina and Aunt Helen that I was there in Radom, forced to work for the Reich.

My work was packing ammunition in boxes. The factory floor was a hell of noise and chemical fumes. Any idea we might have of thwarting our captors was defeated from the start. Our speed and efficiency were checked repeatedly, and the punishment for sabotaging the ammunition was death. There was no appeal. I fell into my bunk every night exhausted and weak from undernourishment and from breathing gunpowder. I was more anaemic than ever. Often, I felt so faint on the factory floor that I caught myself swaying and had to grab the workbench to keep from falling. We were forced to work standing for hours at a time. Workers disappeared regularly, and no-one dared ask what had happened to them. By the time I had been in the factory for two weeks, I was sick and wasted, but I was terrified that if I could not do this terrible job, I would be taken away to something even worse.

One morning, a cadre of officers came to inspect us, and I recognized the major who had chosen us for the factory. As he approached my station, I bent my head to my work, my hands fumbling with the shells I had to bundle, and darkness flooded my vision from the sides until I could not see. I knew I was falling, and I faintly heard the sound of my own body hitting the floor.

When I came to, I was on a couch in an office. The major handed me a cup of coffee.

'*Wie heisst du?*' he asked.

My hands shook as I took the cup. 'My name is Irene Gut.' I noticed his surprise that I had understood German, and that I spoke it well. 'Before the war, I lived in Oberschlesien.'

He took a handkerchief from his pocket and blew his nose. 'You must be of German descent, with that name.'

'I don't know – I don't think so. I am Polish.' I sipped the coffee, which was rich with milk and sugar, luxuries I hadn't tasted in months.

'So, you don't claim to be German – you'd be surprised how many people do,' he said. He gave me a cynical smile. 'I must admire your honesty for not attempting to do so.'

We were both silent for a moment while I drank my coffee. Then he went to his desk and stirred some papers with his forefinger, frowning. 'You are jeopardizing the efficiency of the factory. If you are too sick to work—'

'No, Herr Major! I am not too sick!' I interrupted. I struggled to sit up. 'Please don't deport me. Please let me stay here, where I am close to my sister. I will work harder.'

He did not look at me. He was considering. 'Your German is very good. Perhaps you are wasted on the assembly line.'

I held my breath, trying not to cry.

'I have a job for which you might be better suited, at the officers' mess. Do you have domestic skills? Any experience in a kitchen, and serving food?'

I nearly jumped from the couch. 'Yes, Herr Major! My mother brought us up to be able to do everything in the home, to prepare food and be a good hostess. I can do all those things!'

The major nodded as he began writing. 'Report to Herr Schulz at seven in the morning, at this address. He doesn't speak Polish, and he has been having terrible trouble communicating with the Polish staff. He will be delighted to have you.' He began to hand the pass to me, but kept it out of my reach as I leaned forward. 'I am letting you go to your home, but do not fail to show up or I will send a patrol for you.'

'No, Major,' I breathed. 'I will not be late. I will not disappoint you. Thank you.'

He paused another moment, and then handed me the pass. It was signed Major Eduard Rügemer.

To say that Janina and Aunt Helen were surprised to see me is an understatement. Janina burst into tears and threw her arms around me, and would not let me go for several minutes. While I ate some bread and a carrot, I told them what had happened to me since the Sunday I had been caught in the łapanka. Janina kept hold of my hand and repeatedly brushed tears from her face as I spoke. When I collapsed into bed that night, I felt that I had slid to the edge of an abyss, but someone had dragged me back.

By six-thirty the next morning, I was on my way to my new job. The address Major Rügemer had given me was of an old hotel in the southeast corner of downtown Radom. It was a stately, dignified old place, where once weddings and parties had set the chandeliers jingling with dance music. I turned down the alley at the side of the hotel to the service entrance, and went in.

A stout, red-faced man in a big white apron was just walking to the door with a pail of garbage.

'Yes?'

'I am looking for Herr Schulz,' I said in German.

'You have found him,' he replied, looking me up and down. 'You are my new girl?'

'Yes, Herr Schulz. Irene Gut.'

'Does "Irene" mean "Skinnybones" in Polish, perhaps?'

I blushed. 'Oh, I am sorry,' I stammered. 'I am—'

'Hungry. So, I will feed you. Come this way, Fräulein Skinnybones.'

Warily, hungrily, I followed him back the way he had come, down the corridor and into the huge kitchen. There were piles of good food everywhere: fresh bread – *white* bread – cheeses, fruits, round beets with dirt still clinging to them, baskets of apples, pastries, pots of jam. There were two walk-in refrigerators, which my hungry imagination filled with meat and poultry and tall cans of creamy milk. I had not seen such quantities of food since before the war began.

Herr Schulz began piling a plate, talking to me at the same time. 'I need you to help me with the tradesmen and deliveries,' he explained. 'The Polish language is nothing but gibberish to me – I beg your pardon.'

I lowered myself into a chair at the table, wondering if it could be my hunger that made me believe that Herr Schulz was a friendly, kindly man. He carved a thick slice of bread and balanced it atop my full plate, and then sat and watched me expectantly.

'Eat. Go ahead,' he urged me with a smile.

'You are very – kind,' I said at last, picking up a fork.

He cocked his head to one side. 'So, you think Herr Schulz does not have daughters of his own? Go ahead, dig in.'

I decided I would not question his generosity, but be grateful for it. I managed to give him a quick smile before I attacked my food. For as long as I could remember, I had not eaten enough to be full, but now it looked as though Herr Schulz wished me to be big and fat. I almost cried at my good fortune.

While I tore my bread in half and smeared butter on it, Schulz mixed an egg yolk in a glass of red wine and sugar. 'I see you are not only hungry but perhaps sick, too. This is to build up your blood.'

'Thank you very much, Herr Schulz.'

I soon found out that my impression of him was not wrong. Schulz was a good, friendly man. To be sure, he was in the Wehrmacht, but he was a cook, not a soldier, and he had none of the ferocity and malevolence that I had come to expect of the Germans. And although he was a perfection-ist and liked everything to be done just so, he was quick with praise and gentle with rebukes.

In addition to acting as translator for Schulz, I helped to serve three meals a day in the dining room, where German officers from all over the city gathered for pork chops, roasted chicken, sauerkraut and knockwurst, soufflés, beet soup, chocolate cakes. The amount of food I saw consumed – and left over – in that room sometimes made my head spin, especially when I knew how poorly everyone else was eating. After several weeks, I got up the courage to ask Schulz if I might take some leftovers home for my aunt and my sister, and naturally, he was generous in preparing packages of meat, bread, and vegetables. It made my heart ache with relief when I noticed that Janina was beginning to lose the pinched and hollow look in her face. We still did not hear anything from our parents, but every day we prayed that they sometimes had a chance to eat good food.

Frequently, my work cleaning up after dinner kept me after curfew, especially if there was a party that went on for several hours. Major Rügemer signed passes for me, or allowed Schulz to drive me home. The major was always polite when I served him in the dining room; he remembered my name and asked how my sister was. Dozens of SS and Wehrmacht officers came and went all the time, and they were the usual mixture of men: some loud and crude in their wine, some grave and determined as they talked of the war and ignored their food, others trying to get fresh with the waitresses or German secretaries. Nazi flags hung at each end of the room, and a large photograph of Hitler presided over the tables like the host of a party. The windows of the dining room faced the street; occasionally, I would notice someone pass by and pause for a moment, watching the Germans eat as though it were a rare and exotic spectacle, before turning away and hurrying on.

November came, and with it the cold, the low grey sky,

and the snow. Schulz took me with him to the Wehrmacht's *Warenhaus*, the warehouse stuffed with the contents of countless raided shops and homes, and helped me pick out a pair of warm winter boots so that my walks to and from the old hotel would not freeze my feet. I went to work the next day in good spirits: my feet were warm, the sky was blue, and the snow was as white as the powdered sugar on one of Schulz's sacher tortes. I was almost happy.

'*Guten Morgen*, Fräulein Irene,' Schulz called as I came in, stamping snow from my boots.

'*Dzień dobry*, Pan Schulz,' I replied in Polish.

'Today, I need you to set the tables in the ballroom upstairs for a formal dinner,' he said. He was rolling pastry dough and was dusted with flour up to his elbows. He jerked his chin upward. 'All the silver and linens are there already.'

I tied on my apron and threaded my way through the labyrinthine passages that made up the behind-the-scenes area of the hotel, then up the creaking service elevator to the fourth floor. The plush red carpeting of the upstairs lobby felt soft underfoot, and the daylight sent rainbows from the prisms of the chandeliers. In the ballroom, I walked to a window to let in some more light. The velvet drapes released a slight shower of dust as I threw them open.

I glanced out. The ballroom was at the rear of the hotel, and I realized I had never looked out that side of the building. The view showed me just more city, although I noticed that a wooden fence topped with barbed wire ran directly in back of the hotel. Then I understood. Beyond the barbed wire was the Glinice ghetto.

At first, the place seemed deserted, the way the woods do when you first enter in the winter. In the woods, you see nothing but trees, the tops of creeping plants, shapes muffled by snow. But little by little, you notice a cuckoo dipping its tail in a ray of sunlight, or you hear the footfall of a deer as it paws through the crust to reach moss to eat. The ghetto was the same; at first, it looked like nothing but empty streets dark with scabs of dirty snow and slush. Then, gradually, I began to notice people: two children, hand in hand, picking their way across a patch of ice; an old Hasidic man with side-curls locking a door behind him; a woman carrying a basket across the street.

The brightness faded from my day. I had forgotten the Jews, driven from their homes, crowded into the ghetto. I was sure they were worse off even than the rest of us Poles. I had sometimes overheard officers talking during dinner of the 'Jewish problem', but I had always been too busy working to pay much heed – and to be honest, too worried about my own problems to think about the Jews. Now I berated myself for the good food I had eaten and given my family, for feeling so lucky, so well-fed. I watched the old Hasid, stepping as carefully as a stork through the slush, turn a corner and disappear.

A voice from down the hall made me jump, and I hurried to set the tables. There were dozens of places to set, and for an hour I was busy folding napkins and laying the silver. The hotel was as hushed as a church.

Then, the sound of gunfire broke into the quiet ballroom. Still clutching a handful of knives, I ran to the window to see what on earth was happening.

The scene below me was like an anthill kicked to pieces.

Men, women, and children were running through the streets. SS men were spilling out of trucks and shooting at the fleeing Jews. Bodies were sprawled in the slush. Through the glass I heard faint screams and the frenzied barking of police dogs. The snow darkened with blood. I was squeezing the knives so sharply that one of them bit into my hand, and when I dropped them they clattered loudly on the floor. I stared at my hand, where a thin line of blood welled up from a cut. It was not real. This could not be real. I looked from my hand to the scene of murder outside and felt a scream rising in me as though I had been shot myself.

A hand clamped down over my mouth. I whirled around, struggling. Schulz was holding on to me, shaking his head. He was deathly pale.

'Be quiet, Irene!'

He took his hand away to pull the drapes shut and dragged me away from the window.

'Schulz! What is happening?' I wailed. I was nearly hysterical, and tried to go back to see.

He pressed my hands between his and forced me to look at him. There was a line of sweat on his upper lip. 'Don't, Irene. You never saw this.'

'But they're kill—'

'Don't speak of it to anyone. Don't cry – they will think you are a Jew-lover.'

I stared at him. I could not understand what he was saying.

'Irene. Bad things happen to Jew-lovers. Do you understand me? Very bad.'

Slowly, slowly, I nodded. My neck felt stiff and rusty, as though it might break.

Schulz sent a nervous glance at the door. I could feel his hands trembling even as he tried to control mine, and he was breathing unevenly.

'You won't be fit to serve today,' he whispered. 'Go home. I will say – I will say that you are sick. But you must come back tomorrow at the usual time. And you must tell yourself you never saw this. Now go.'

He shook me slightly, and then pushed me toward the door. 'Go.'

I had just seen the Germans' answer to their 'Jewish problem'.

A Drop in the Ocean

When I returned to work the next day, I could not look at
Schulz. As good and kind as he was, he was a German, and
I could not reconcile those two things in my mind. I was so
confused and heartsick that I could barely speak. I went
about my duties with the deadness of a machine. My skin
prickled constantly throughout the day, as though the
presence of the ghetto beyond the hotel was making itself
known to me. I had to do something.

During the afternoon, while cleaning up from lunch, I
found myself alone in the kitchen. It was the chance I had
been waiting for. I took a pail of garbage from the floor
beside me and stepped out into the alley. The alley ran from
the street along the side of the hotel, dead-ending at a fence.
The ghetto, I now knew, was on the other side. I glanced
quickly out towards the street; cars passed, and two women
walked by, muffled in heavy coats, but nobody looked my
way.

I walked to the fence. It was made of boards, with coils
of barbed wire attached to metal posts and curved spikes at
the top. Through the boards I could see the continuation
of the alley on the other side, and the backs of two apartment houses. I glanced over my shoulder again, and then
examined the ground under the fence. The alleyway was
packed dirt, hard with frost.

I took a large metal cooking spoon from my apron pocket and knelt down. I scraped at the dirt. The sound echoed loudly off the sides of the buildings, making my heart race. Not a face showed at a window. Not a footstep. Nothing.

I gripped the spoon tighter, scraping and gouging at the ground until I had made a small hole, about the size of a loaf of bread, under the fence. From the pail I removed a layer of potato peelings, and took out a tin box I had filled with cheese and apples. I wedged that in the hole, and then hurried back to the kitchen. 'Whoever helps a Jew shall be punished by death' was the warning I had heard over and over. It was written on posters. It was broadcast from loud-speakers on the street. 'Whoever helps a Jew shall be punished by death.'

The next morning, I looked for the box. It was empty.

My heart thudded in my ears as I picked up the box. I had put food on the ground, and was now in danger of capital punishment. Without looking back, I entered the kitchen, and went back to work for the Nazis.

Every day now, I found a chance to slip outside and leave food under the fence. I knew it was a drop in the ocean, but I could not do nothing. I never saw anyone on the ghetto side. I never lingered. I did not want to see anyone, nor did I want anyone to see me. In spite of what I was doing, my first concern was for Janina: she was my responsibility. I could not take any risk that would be a risk to her.

And that was why, when she lost her job, I was torn about what to do. I wanted to have her with me, working at the hotel, where I could look out for her. But I did not want her to know the truth about what was happening, did not want her exposed to the conversation of the Nazi officers. I could not decide which was the lesser of two evils.

In the meantime, however, we had news that made my decision for me. A former neighbour of ours from Kozłowa Góra showed up on Aunt Helen's doorstep one day between Christmas and New Year's. Peter was dressed in a German uniform, and was on his way to the front: he had been conscripted into the army. The sight of him in uniform depressed me, but I was anxious for news of our family. Peter handed me a letter, and when I begged him to wait, in case I had any questions he could answer, he looked nervous.

'It won't look good for me or you,' he muttered, lighting a cigarette with red, chapped hands.

We stayed on the steps in the icy air while I read Mamusia's letter. It was on flimsy, tissuelike paper, so thin that the ink had bled through and the pen had torn it. But I held it steady in the wind and read it as fast as my tears would allow.

'We are all together, but the girls are being worked as slaves in the clay mines . . . We must all wear an armband with the letter "P" for "Pole," on it . . . The Germans will not let Tatuś leave, and I am afraid, my dear girls, that we will not be reunited until this war is over.'

I let out a groan, thinking of my little sisters working in the mines, in the cold, in the wet, covered with mud like animals. I pressed one hand to my chin to keep it from trembling.

'I have to go,' Peter said.

I grabbed his arm. 'Have you seen them? Are they—'

'They're alive. I must go.'

I hugged my collar around my neck as he walked away. The gate banged shut behind him.

To my mind, the matter was settled. I must have Janina close to me. I could not bear the thought of being separated from her. If she worked with me, I could keep my eye on her and possibly protect her from some of the horror that the world had become. The next day I asked Schulz, telling him how skilled and capable Janina was, and he readily agreed to put her on the staff, a decision he was authorized to make. So the new year of 1942 arrived, and Janina began working at my side in the officers' dining hall, standing lookout for me when I put my tin box under the ghetto fence.

It was at the beginning of the year also that Schulz told me the entire operation would be moving east in April. The eastern front was being pushed deep into Russian territory, and the Germans were pressing the advantage. The munitions factory would relocate to be closer to the fighting, and we – the domestic staff – would be going, too. For this reason, I was even happier that Janina was now working with me. We would be moved together.

We would be moving in the spring. To Ternopol. I couldn't believe my ears when Schulz told me our destination. It seemed I had done nothing for the last two springs but try to leave Ternopol, and here I was going back again! I had no fear that my old persecutors would be there: that part of the Ukraine was now firmly under the control of the Germans. But I didn't know whether to laugh or cry at the irony of it. It was springtime; it was time to return to Ternopol.

In the meantime, the number of officers who came for meals every day increased with the escalation in the war effort. A new factory facility was under construction, and

Major Rügemer awaited daily reports from the building site to the east. A feeling of expectancy filled the dining room during each meal, and the buzz of talk was like the hum of machinery.

Often, dinner conversation would come to a standstill as someone tuned the radio to listen to a speech from Berlin; as Hitler's voice broke like hail upon the china and crystal, Janina and I would exchange quick looks and tiptoe away with our heavy trays. The Bolsheviks, enemies of the Reich, would be crushed! – the manic voice would shout – And the Jews, who were in league with the Bolsheviks, would feel the heels of the invincible Wehrmacht on their necks!

To us, these speeches sounded bizarre and grotesque; they were the spit and vomit of a madman. And yet, the officers would be turned to Hitler's portrait at the end of the room, listening transfixed, as though to the words of their saviour. I thought of the poor Jews I had seen shot down, and I wondered how the officers could believe that old men in prayer shawls, mothers with children, fathers plying their trades could be dangerous enemies.

But obviously, they did. One morning in March, when Janina and I arrived at work, we saw bulldozers crawling across the rubble that had been the ghetto. Here and there among the broken masonry and the shattered window frames I noticed a crushed hat, a burst suitcase, a silver candlestick. Janina and I tried not to make it obvious that we were watching as we scurried past the noise and destruction. A Gestapo officer paced back and forth along the sidewalk like a dog guarding a bone. I felt for Janina's hand and gripped it tight. She was pale with grief, and I felt, myself, as though I had lost someone dear; an announcement was being trumpeted with great pride from the loudspeaker at the corner of the street: 'This town is Jew-free!'

But it Was Not a Bird

By the time we were to move, Radom had become unbearable to me. It was now impossible *not* to understand what Hitler's plans for the Jews were, and every day that I had to pass the demolished ghetto opened the wound afresh. Sometimes, at night, Janina and I would recall Jewish friends from our girlhood, remembering the trouble we got into when we snuck out at night to attend a party, or the laughs we had falling into the lily pond near Tatuś' factory. David, Aaron, Rachel, Ruth – friends who were Jewish but who were not different from us. It seemed to us, as we lay sleepless in the dark, that if our childhood friends could be considered enemies, what was to keep us from the same fate? Weren't we all the same? Hitler would finish the Jews, ghetto by ghetto, and then turn his full attention to the rest of us Poles.

I was sorry to say farewell to Aunt Helen, but I did not regret leaving Radom. I did not expect to find life different anywhere else, however. We were sent east by truck to Lvov; the new factory in Ternopol was not yet ready, but it was necessary to move our operations closer to the Russian front.

Janina and I packed; our luggage was one suitcase for the two of us. As the convoy of trucks bounced and bucked over the potholed roads, we watched the countryside go past. April had poured streams of wild flowers between the furrows of the farmland: the yellow *kaczeniec*, blue forget-me-not, pink primroses. But much of the farmland was fallow, abandoned by peasants on the run from the war, or left idle by farmers who were themselves fighting in the war. At this time of year, there should have been a pale green haze like a lacy scarf lying over the rich land, but there were few fields where the wheat was coming up. Food would grow scarce that fall, obviously, but I knew it wouldn't be the Germans going hungry.

Our temporary barracks in Lvov was another converted hotel. Now, close to the front, our outfit's staff grew, and I was kept on the run constantly – before, during, and after every meal. Janina's job was to act as housekeeper for the German officers' and secretaries' rooms. Our schedule left us little extra time. My birthday, May 5, came and went with little to make it different from every other busy day, except that Janina surprised me with a bouquet of lilacs, which perfumed the kitchen and reminded us of old, sweet times.

I was twenty now, and it seemed as though half my life had been wartime. Sometimes I felt like an old woman. I had seen terrible things, and terrible things had been done to me. Often – such as when a German officer made some rude, suggestive comment, or when I saw a child in the street who looked particularly thin and hungry – often I felt a great welling up of hatred and rebellion. It was not right, what I had seen, and what had been done to me, and what I saw around me every day. In God's name, it was not right! And yet I was relatively safe. I was well fed. I had my sister with me. I knew that most people were not as well off as I was. If I felt so much anger and outrage, what must other people not so fortunate be feeling? Surely, the evil being done in my country must be a poison that would ruin the soil, tarnish the air, and foul the water. Sometimes, when I thought of the amount of hatred dwelling in Poland, I was surprised to see that the grass was still green, that the trees still flourished their leaves against a blue sky.

And yet they did. It is a terrible irony of war, that nature itself does not rebel when man turns against his brother. I have seen nightmares take place on beautiful spring days. The birds can hop from one branch to another, tipping their heads and honing their small beaks against the bark while a child dies in the mud below.

From time to time – when there was time – these thoughts led me to church. One Sunday, Janina and I found ourselves walking out at the end of the mass with a young Polish woman and her mother. We exchanged greetings, and seeing that it was a beautiful day, and that our paths lay together for some distance, we took a stroll together, which brought us to a park. The young woman introduced herself as we paused by a duck pond.

'My name is Helen Weinbaum, and this is my mother, Pani Klimeka.'

'*Dzień dobry*, 'Janina said with a sunny smile. 'It is such a pleasure to meet you. I am Janina Gutowna, and this is my big sister, Irena.'

'How nice to speak Polish!' I said. 'We work for the Germans – their language sounds harsh, no matter what you say.'

'Have you always lived in Lvov?' Janina asked.

Helen and her mother exchanged a sad look, and

Helen patted the older woman's shoulder.

'No. We used to live in Krasnoe, but my – my father was killed by the Gestapo in a reprisal because someone slashed the tyres of the commandant's car. And my husband, Henry, was taken to a work camp for Jews near here. I have tried to get permission to visit him at the *Arbeitslager*; but so far it is not allowed.'

Helen absently tore a handful of leaves from an overhanging branch as she spoke, dropping them one by one into the water as she mentioned each thing that had befallen her family. The ripples spread out from each leaf, gliding away endlessly. She was lucky, if you could call it luck, that they had not arrested her along with her husband. Helen was not Jewish, but she fervently swore she wished she were: at least then she would be with her beloved Henry in the *Arbeitslager*.

In turn, Janina and I told of our own misfortunes, and of how we had come to be in Lvov. Everyone in Poland in those days had a bitter story. Everyone. Our tales made a bond between us; we parted company that day as good friends, and Janina and I promised to visit Helen and her mother in their cottage outside of town when we could, and to bring food, because they had so little.

We did visit with them often as the spring progressed, and I began to feel I had another sister. There were times when Helen and Janina and I could laugh and act as if there were no war; but then something would remind Helen of her Henry, and her laughter would stick in her throat.

As the weeks followed each other into the summer, more and more of the officers and secretaries went on ahead to Ternopol; our work became much lighter, and we had more time off to spend with our new friends. One Sunday in July, we found Helen and her mother in a state of barely controlled hysteria. They had heard a rumour that a large number of Jews from the *Arbeitslagers* and from surrounding shtetls had been rounded up by the SS and were being held in a nearby village. Helen begged us to go with her, to see if she could find Henry among them.

Janina and I did not have to confer. The four of us hitched a ride on a farmer's wagon and were soon in town, at the bus station. There were dozens of people waiting for the same bus, and from the bits and pieces of overheard conversation, we knew that most of them were on the same fearful errand.

As we waited in the sun for our bus, rumour snuck like a pickpocket through the crowd, stealing the hope from people's hearts. At first, only isolated words stood out against the general murmur: camps. Disappeared. All. Death squads. Then we heard whole phrases: burned the synagogue. Shot the men. Orders from Berlin. One by one, these words and phrases fitted into each other like pieces of a jigsaw puzzle. Somewhere a woman let out a wail. An old man called out to God. Helen was staring ahead at the street, as though forcing the bus to arrive by her own will. I saw that she was holding her mother's hand, and then realized that I was holding Janina's hand. Wherever Henry Weinbaum was, he was in danger: he was in the hands of the SS. We might find him at the end of our journey. We might not.

All of us in that crowd were fearful of what lay ahead, and yet when the bus finally came wheezing and grinding its gears down the street, we rushed forward as one body. The bus filled. It pulled away. We were all on it.

There was very little talk as the bus made its way to our destination. There was nothing to say. When we arrived, we climbed down onto the hot pavement, and as if by some secret signal, like a flock of sparrows wheeling away across a church square, we all moved in one direction.

It was in the marketplace. The whole square had been fenced off. Behind the barbed wire stood hundreds of people whose yellow stars marked them as Jews. Trucks were unloading scores more, and as each man, woman, or child jumped down, bewildered and frightened, the black-uniformed SS men sorted them roughly: women and children one way, old men another, young men towards another mass of trucks. Outside the fence, friends and family members pressed against the wire, calling out names, crowding for a glimpse of a loved one.

'I don't see him! How will I find him?' Helen wailed, standing on her toes and looking frantically one way and then another.

Suddenly, several of the guards strode towards the fence, shouting at the crowd. *'Raus! Raus verfluchte Schweine!'* One of them slung the gun off his shoulder and began shooting into the air.

There were screams on our side of the wire, and people stumbled into one another. Some would not be chased away, but kept pressing forward. The man with the gun levelled it at us, and we broke in panic. We were all running, but when I heard Janina cry out, I turned to help her.

'I've twisted my ankle!' she gasped, struggling to her feet.

Helen and I took her arms, and the four of us dodged

through the crowd to a row of buildings lining the square. We slipped down an alley, and I found a door that stood ajar. Putting my shoulder to it, I shoved it wide, and we all hurried inside.

It was a house. It was someone's house, but no-one lived there now: furniture was broken, scattered across the floor. Broken dishes and glassware lay in piles, and dark squares on the wallpaper showed where pictures and paintings had been taken down.

'This is a Jewish home,' Helen said, turning around and around amid the wreckage. 'This house has been raided.'

We heard more shouts and pounding footsteps on the street outside. Without speaking, we ran up the stairs and into a front bedroom. Janina hobbled to a window, and stood with her back to the wall so she could peek out sideways. We all did the same. We did not speak, but our hard breathing was loud in the empty room.

Below in the marketplace, the SS men had lined up facing the Jews, their guns gleaming in the sun. *'Raus, Schweinhundjude! Schnell! Schnell!'* Out, Jewish pigs! Fast! Fast!

The gates were dragged open, and the Jewish prisoners were forced out through a gauntlet, while the guards beat at them with their rifle butts. An old man, tottering with a cane, was not fast enough, and a guard shot him on the spot. In vain, women tried to protect their small children from blows, men tried to shield their old fathers. But every time someone stumbled and fell under the beatings, shots rang out. The street was paved with bodies, and still the Jews were forced to march out over them.

We watched this from our windows in a paralysis of

horror. We could do nothing but watch. We could not even pull back from the glass to keep hidden. An old rabbi carrying the Torah stopped to help a young woman with a shrieking toddler, and all three were shot. A greybeard in a faded uniform of the Polish army from the last war limped past the guards, and he, too, was not fast enough. The sun shone down on all of them, and the dust settled in pools of blood.

By this time, the four of us were crying uncontrollably. Helen was on her knees, sobbing in her mother's arms. Janina turned her face away. But I watched, flattening myself against the window. As I pressed against the glass, I saw an officer make a flinging movement with his arm, and something rose up into the sky like a fat bird. With his other hand he aimed his pistol, and the bird plummeted to the ground beside its screaming mother, and the officer shot the mother, too.

But it was not a bird. It was not a bird. It was not a bird.

When the long march of prisoners had filed down the road out of town, we crept from our hiding place. Already, trucks had cleared the street of corpses; flies buzzed and hovered over the stains congealing on the cobblestones. Like frightened children lost in a forest, we scurried from one shadow to another, startling at every sound, our hearts pounding with fear and dismay. We did not need to say to one another, 'We must see where the Nazis are taking those people.' We simply followed, as soon as we dared.

And yet, before we had reached the outskirts of town, we began to hear shooting. We flattened ourselves against the wall of a garage, and with each crackling wave of gunfire, we flinched as though we were being shot ourselves. The shooting continued for a long time – a very long time – and when it finally was over, we left, again without speaking, for the bus station. We walked like dead women, our souls crushed.

We did not speak of what we had seen. At the time, to speak of it seemed worse than sacrilege: we had witnessed a thing so terrible that it acquired a dreadful holiness. It was a miracle of evil. It was not possible to say with words what we had witnessed, and so we kept it safely guarded until the time when we could bring it out, and show it to others, and say, 'Behold. This is the worst thing man can do.'

Only a Girl

Now it was August. The German offensive line had pushed
east, and the city of Stalingrad was under steady attack. By
the middle of the month, we were in Ternopol, where the
new factory was churning out truckloads of ammunition
every week. The complex was called Harres-Krafa Park, or
HKP, and it took up nearly three city blocks. A four-storey
hotel had been converted into suites for the officers; on
the first floor were a dining hall, a smaller private dining
room, a service kitchen, and a recreation room. Another
building had been renovated into suites for the secretaries,
and across the compound was a large barracks for
the soldiers who worked in the factory. Next to that were
the main kitchen and mess hall, in their own building; to
the right was a machine repair shop, and on the left
was a one-storey building that housed the laundry and
mending shop. Taking up one side of the complex was the
factory itself, and around the entire facility ran a fence, with
guardhouses at regular intervals. Janina and I shared
a small room beside the service kitchen in the main
building.

As before, my duties were primarily in the dining hall
and kitchen, and Janina's were in the officers' and secretaries' bedroom suites. Meals were prepared in the large
kitchen across the compound, and large pots and platters

were brought to the service kitchen in the officers' dining hall. From that smaller kitchen I served the officers' meals, and it was there that I cleaned up afterwards. There were at least thirty-five people at each meal, and often more, so the preparation and clean-up kept Schulz and me busy most of the day. I also helped Janina when I could spare some time. But even with all that work, Schulz gave me an additional job within the first week of our arrival. He put me in charge of the laundry facility, where I would oversee the washing and mending of the officers' and secretaries' clothes.

Like the factory, the laundry used Jewish workers from the local *Arbeitslager*, the work camp. The Jews were trucked in daily and were counted before being sent to their work. On the first day that I entered the laundry room, I met my staff of twelve men and women.

They were wary of me at first, assuming that I was German, but I did my best to reassure them. They had all once been individuals of means. One had been a successful businessman, one a medical student, one a lawyer. One woman had been a dressmaker, and one had been a nurse. For the most part, they were German Jews who had been deported to the east. Some had families in the Ternopol ghetto, but seldom had a chance to see them. Life in the *Arbeitslager* was a misery.

'Sometimes Sturmbannführer Rokita forces us to stand outside the barracks for hours after a full day of work,' Ida Haller told me.

'If anyone moves or makes a noise, they're beaten, or sometimes shot,' added her husband, Lazar.

A woman my own age named Fanka Silberman was

working the handle of the wringer, squeezing the water from a sheet. 'But at least we are better off here than in the ghetto. We are the strong ones, the ones who can work. As long as Rokita does not single us out for punishment.'

'Who is this Rokita?' I asked them.

Herschl Morris glanced nervously at the door. 'He is the Sturmbannführer – the battalion commander of the SS here. I think he has nothing but ice where his heart should be.'

I, too, could not help glancing at the door. Their words gave me a chill. 'I'll bring you food when I can. I can hide it in laundry baskets.' I looked at them all, pale and emaciated from years now of hunger. 'I'll look after you.'

Moses Steiner, a stooped and gloomy man, made a small shrug. 'You're only a young girl. What can you do?'

'Hush, Steiner,' Ida hissed.

I put my hand on the man's arm and waited for him to look at me. Reluctantly, he raised his head to meet my gaze. 'Trust me,' I said. 'I will look after you.'

I left the laundry room with a smile, hoping that I had given them courage. But the moment I closed the door behind me, I felt drained. Steiner was right. I was only a girl, alone among the enemy. What could I do?

That night at dinner I brought a platter heaped with sauerbraten to the major's table, and found him deep in conversation with an SS officer I had not seen before. He turned his head to look at me as I approached, and I felt a knock of surprise: he was one of the most handsome men I had ever seen, with gleaming blond hair and eyes the colour of the sky. He looked about thirty years old.

'Good evening, Fräulein Gut,' Major Rügemer said politely. He blew his nose before reaching for the silver serving fork. 'Do you know Sturmbannführer Rokita?'

My throat squeezed shut for a moment. I set the platter down carefully. 'Good – good evening, sir,' I stammered, careful not to look at Rokita. I focused instead on the swastika armband around his left sleeve, and then noticed the silver death's-head ring on his hand. I trembled in spite of myself.

'What a pretty girl, Major,' Rokita said. 'And what an old dog you are.'

Major Rügemer flushed. 'Don't be absurd, Rokita.'

I stood there, feeling like a prize mare, hot with embarrassment. Coming upon the cruel SS chief unexpectedly had rattled me.

'Fräulein Gut, I don't bite,' Rokita teased.

I glanced at him, appalled. Was he flirting with me? Did he think I was blushing because I wanted him to like me?

'Excuse me, Herr Major. I have other tables.'

'Of course, of course, Fräulein Gut. Thank you.'

I walked stiffly away under the manic gaze of Hitler's picture, and retreated to the service kitchen, where Schulz was busy opening bottles of wine. I had seen the head of the SS, and I had no doubt that what Herschl Morris said was true: Rokita had a heart of ice. Those blue eyes were cold, without life, and the ring on his hand was like a mirror of his soul. To be under his command must be as dangerous as living below a snowfield: one false move, and the ice would come down and crush you. He was a powerful enemy. He was my enemy, and I would try to thwart him.

'Herr Schulz,' I began, 'do you suppose I can get extra help? It is so much work to handle the meals and the laundry, and also help Janina with the rooms.'

Schulz wiped his hands on his big apron and sniffed the neck of a wine bottle. 'Let me talk to the major, Irene. Perhaps he can give you some women from the factory.'

'What a good thought,' I said, as though surprised. 'Why don't I get some recommendations from the laundry workers? They might know some reliable people.'

'I'll speak to the major.'

I loaded a tray with dishes of potatoes, gave Schulz a smile, and hoisted the tray to my hip. It was a start.

And so two days later, I was given ten more workers, all friends or relatives of the people in the laundry room. I took eight of the new people, all women, to the secretaries' building, where my sister was cleaning.

'This is Janina. She is in charge of you and she will help you,' I said. 'Find something to do. Look busy all the time. You are better off here than in the factory or the *Arbeitslager* or the ghetto. You will be able to stay here all day, every day, if you manage it right. And we'll feed you.'

'We thought it was something terrible when our names were called,' one woman said. 'We were so frightened.'

Janina took the woman's hand. 'Don't be. Irene is my big sister. She will look out for you.'

I sent Janina a grateful smile, and hurried back to the kitchen to begin training my two new helpers from the camp, Roman and Sozia.

Steiner was right: I was only a girl. Nobody paid much attention to me. While I served dinners in the evenings, I came and went among the officers and I was an invisible servant, a pair of hands bringing and removing plates. The officers talked as if I were not there: I did not count. I was only a girl.

But I listened to the officers discuss the progress at the front. I listened to the secretaries gossip about Berlin. I listened especially when Rokita dined with Major Rügemer, which was quite often, and if he thought I lingered because I had a crush on him, so much the better.

'How do you manage such efficiency, Rokita?' the major asked one evening.

Rokita's cupid's-bow mouth curved in a sneer. 'Training, Major. I have trained the Jews well. No one is lazy, I can promise you that. I am very good at discipline.'

'But not to the point that they cannot work, I assume?' Rügemer asked, spreading butter on a hot roll. 'This factory is important to the war effort. I don't want my workers abused.'

'Don't worry. But if on Thursday you discover that some workers have been replaced, it is because they were . . . lazy. You will be better off without them.'

In the morning, I reported the conversation to the workers in the laundry. 'Expect trouble tomorrow,' I said. 'A raid or something. Spread the word if you can.'

And in this way, I made my weakness my advantage. If I happened to overhear plans for a raid on the ghetto, it never showed on my face. If I passed a table when a disciplinary action was being scheduled for the *Arbeitslager*, no one suspected I cared. And when Rokita came to dine, I was always polite to him, and let him flatter himself that I lingered by his table because I was awed by his beauty and his power.

After all, I was only a girl.

Stealing from Rokita

Perhaps three times a week, Rokita came to dine with Major Rügemer. Frequently, he was on the road, 'cleaning up' the ghettos around that part of the Ukraine, as he put it. Ultimately, Rokita's job was to make the Ukraine *judenrein*, Jew-free. The Jews who could work were exploited to the end of their usefulness. Then they were rounded up and sent away – we did not know where. The 'excess' population of the ghetto was removed – and were not heard from ever again.

Whatever I overheard from Rokita, I passed along to my friends in the laundry room. Lazar Haller, who had become their spokesman, decided how best to communicate with the ghetto. There were spy networks among the Jews, that was obvious. In spite of brutal security, reports and messages did pass between the *Arbeitslager* and the ghetto; some of the prisoners in the *Arbeitslager* were allowed to visit family in the ghetto. When we knew of a planned *Aktion*, some people escaped to live in the forests, or hid before the raid.

But this was only possible if we knew ahead of time. Rokita did not mention all of his plans to Major Rügemer, and I was not able to hover nearby all the time. Sometimes there were *Aktions* of which we had no warning, and I knew, when I went to the laundry room and saw the tears on my friends' faces, that Rokita had struck again in the night.

One sunny September morning after breakfast, I entered the laundry room to find Ida Haller crying inconsolably in her husband's arms. The others were at work, their faces pale. I looked from one to another, and then my stomach rolled over.

'Where is Fanka?' I asked.

Clara Bauer's hands were shaking as she tried to thread a needle. 'She had a pass to visit her parents last night. She did not return – we think, we are afraid—'

'There may have been a raid,' Abram Klinger broke in.

I backed up, step by step, blindly searching for something to brace myself against. I bumped into the door frame, and then spun around and stumbled out into the sunshine again. Soldiers were loading crates onto a truck in the centre of the compound, laughing and joking with one another as they hoisted the ammunition. Atop the flagpole, the Nazi flag flapped and curled in a lazy breeze. From an open kitchen window came a clatter of pots and pans, and then Schulz's voice raised in a song.

I pressed my fists against my chin for a moment, trying to control my racing thoughts. I had to find Fanka Silberman – if she was still alive. Across the compound, the windowpanes of the factory reflected the autumn sunshine. I hurried across the hard-packed earth and went into the factory offices.

'I must see Major Rügemer right away,' I said to his secretary.

She looked at me coldly. 'What is it about?'

I fought hard to remain calm. 'I must see Major Rügemer right away,' I repeated.

The door to his office was open, and I heard the major's chair scrape backward. 'Fräulein Gut? You may come in.

His secretary sniffed and went back to her work as I hurried into the major's office.

'Herr Major, one of my workers was mending some dresses for the secretaries and took them with her to the ghetto to use a special machine at the tailor's shop. She did not come back.'

Rügemer yanked off his glasses and scowled at the papers on his desk. I could see his jaw working as he clenched his teeth. 'Rokita,' he muttered.

'Let me go to the ghetto to look for her and bring the secretaries' dresses back,' I pleaded, coming around to his chair.

He continued scowling at his desk, motionless for a moment. Then he pulled open a drawer and took out a pass. Before he shut it again, I saw that the drawer contained a whole stack of passes, all signed with both his name and Rokita's.

'Here,' Rügemer said, writing my name on the pass. 'Don't be gone long. You have work to do.'

I blurted out my thanks and ran back to the laundry room. 'Ida, tell me how to find the Silbermans' house,' I said, pulling cleaned and ironed dresses willy-nilly from their hangers and stuffing them into a laundry basket. I memorized the directions she gave me, then hurried out again, leaving the laundry workers staring in surprise.

It was a long walk to the ghetto. I was stopped twice and asked for my pass, and each time, I explained that I was on orders from Major Rügemer. At last, I arrived at the gate-house guarding the entrance to the ghetto. Two more soldiers examined my pass.

'I am Major Rügemer's housekeeper,' I said in an imperious tone. 'The dressmaker is here and was supposed to finish these dresses. She has several others with her and the major is very anxious that he have the factory's dressmaker back.'

'*Bitte schön*, Fräulein, go ahead,' one of them said as he opened the gate.

I stepped through, and entered the ghetto. The streets were deserted. From time to time, I caught a glimpse of movement behind a curtain or a shade, and I thought I heard a door close somewhere, but otherwise the place was silent, and my footsteps echoed off the walls of the buildings. I could hear my own blood. The rough wicker of the basket bit into my fingers as I gripped it. I stepped over a book lying face up on the sidewalk where it had been dropped. The Hebrew characters swam together in my vision.

The door of the Silbermans' house was not locked. I pushed it open slowly, and stepped inside. The house was dark, the windows shuttered.

'Fanka? Fanka, please be here. It's Irene.'

There was no answer.

I walked slowly to the staircase, and peered up into the gloom. I prayed she had found time to hide. 'Fanka?' I took a step up.

A hand grabbed my ankle, and I let out a hoarse cry, staring down wildly.

Fanka had hidden in a closet under the stairs. She

crouched in the opening, one arm stuck up through the spindles of the staircase. I dropped the basket and took her hand, pulling her upright. Her eyes were huge with panic.

'Fanka, Fanka, it's me.'

'Irene. Irene, my family. My family is gone! I hid in the basement when I heard the trucks, but my parents—' She began to wail, and I hurried down the step and around to where she stood, and wrapped my arms around her.

'Hush. Hush, Fanka. No noise,' I whispered against her ear.

She clung to me, crying silently, and we stood there in the empty house, crying together. But we could not allow ourselves that solace for long. I pulled away from her and took her by the arms.

'I want to die,' she said brokenly. 'I will stay here and I will die. I should not have hidden. I should have stayed with them.'

'Fanka, listen to me. You must not say that. You must live for them. Come with me.'

I picked up the basket again and piled the tumbled dresses in it, then pulled Fanka with me out of the house. She followed without a word.

'Walk behind me,' I told her. I shoved the basket into her arms. 'Do this for your family, Fanka. You must live.'

At the gate, Fanka stood with downcast eyes as the guards examined the basket. I spoke roughly to her, as though to an inferior.

'Hurry up. Don't dawdle.'

Her head bowed even more, and for a moment I thought she might break down. But I strode through the gate without a backward glance, praying that she would follow me and keep up her part.

After a block, I looked back. Fanka was behind me, tears rolling down her face. 'Just keep walking,' I said in a low voice. 'Please, Fanka. Just keep walking.'

We reached Harres-Krafa Park, and again showed my permit to the guards, and in a few minutes I was leading Fanka back to the laundry room. When I opened the door, all eyes turned toward me, and then Ida and Clara both cried out, rushing forward to take Fanka in their arms. I backed out and shut the door.

Rokita stole Fanka's family. But he did not steal Fanka. I swore he never would.

That night I dreamed I was walking over autumn harvest lands that were heavy with wheat. It was a beautiful red-gold, the colour of Mamusia's amber beads, and overhead was a sky so clear and blue that it was painful to behold. The dried wheat stalks whispered against my legs as I brushed past, and I looked down to see that the ripe and fruitful grains were scattering onto the dirt with a sound like a sigh. I bent to pick them, one by one, from the earth, and place them in my gathered apron, but even as I did, the wind stirred itself and began waving its hand over the fields, strewing the grain. As far as the horizon, the wind was casting the wheat aside, and I felt a wave of panic rise up in me. I picked faster, grabbing up spilled grain by the handful, my nails caked with mud and my loaded apron tugging at my waist until I thought it would drag me down and bury me in the dirt.

Falling from My Hands

The autumn progressed. In the laundry room, my new friends were gaining weight thanks to the food I had been smuggling them every day. They also began turning a wall of shelves into a false front, in case it ever became necessary to hide in the laundry room. As the weather turned cold, I began to worry about them, shivering in their thin summer clothes.

'Herr Schulz,' I began one day as we were cleaning up from breakfast. I was busy scrubbing at some dried egg on a plate and did not look at him. 'Wasn't it cold last night? I wonder if Janina and I could have extra blankets for our beds.'

I glanced at him from the corner of my eye. He, too, was looking down at his work, and frowning slightly. Then he dried his hands and left the kitchen. I continued working, wondering what his abrupt and silent departure meant. He was ordinarily noisy and full of bustle.

When he returned a few minutes later, he carried a tall stack of blankets in his arms – many more than just two extra blankets. 'Irene, if you need anything – anything at all – you must not be afraid to ask me,' he said in a low voice.

At once, my heart began hammering behind my ribs, and my face felt hot, as though I had been caught at something. He knew. Schulz knew what I was doing.

'After all,' he continued in his usual cheerful tone, 'I can't have my girls shivering now, can I? That would reduce our efficiency.'

Confusing emotions chased one another through my heart. I was grateful, and I was relieved, and yet I was almost angry at Schulz for being so kind and for helping me help the Jews without admitting it – he made hating the Germans a complex matter, when it should have been such a straightforward one. Fighting tears, I smiled my thanks and took the blankets away.

When I brought them to the laundry room, Ida and Fanka fell upon them at once, cutting them up to tailor into winter coats. I left them to their work, and found the first snowflakes of winter spiralling down from a dull grey sky as I crossed the compound again to the kitchen.

Rokita now came to dine with Major Rügemer nearly every night. They often drank together in the private dining room after dessert, while some of the other officers played billiards in the recreation room. The air would be thick with cigarette smoke while I moved quietly from room to room, emptying ashtrays, taking away dirty glasses and empty bottles. I gathered whatever information I could to the accompaniment of clicking billiard balls.

But as December began, there was little conversation about anything but the holiday party plans. The officers and secretaries discussed the upcoming celebration with the dedication of students planning a dance. Officially, the Nazi party was not Christian. They had no organized religion, unless you counted their fanatical veneration of Adolf Hitler. However, not everyone was a member of the Nazi party, and the enlisted Wehrmacht soldiers in

The Gut sisters, 1933, Czestochowa. From left to right: Irene, Janina, Marysia, Bronia and Władzia.

Irene at age 15 with Lalka, 1937, Kozłowa Góra.

Irene at age 17 as a nursing student, 1939, Radom.

The Gut sisters, 1941, Radom. From left to right: Władzia, Irene, Marysia, Bronia, and Janina.

Janina and Irene, 1941, Radom.

Outside the ammunition factory dining hall, 1941, Radom.
Irene is on the far right.

Some of the officers'
suites and part of the
gate at Harres-Krafa
Park, 1942, Ternopol.

Irene, 1943, Puszcza
Janówka.

Major Rügemer's villa, 1943, Ternopol. From left to right: the major's secretary; Helen Weinbaum; Pani Klimeka, Helen's mother; and Irene.

Irene on a dorożka, 1943, headed for Puszcza Janówka.

Irene, 1943, at Harres-Krafa Park, Ternopol.

Irene, Herschl, and Pola Morris, 1945, Kraków. Irene is wearing a suit that Herschl made for her.

Reunion, 1945, Kraków. From left to right: Marian Wilner, Fanka Silberman, Henry Weinbaum, Alex Rosen, Pola Morris, Irene, and Moses Steiner.

Irene (with her hair dyed black), Marian Wilner, and Fanka
Silberman, end of 1945, Kraków.

Marian Wilner, after the war.

Fanka Silberman, after the war.

Lazar, Ida, and Roman Haller,
circa 1948.

Major Eduard Rügemer, 1949,
Munich.

Ida Haller, Eduard Rügemer, Pola Lifshitz, 1949, Munich.

Irene and William
Opdyke on their
wedding day,
November 14, 1956.

Wedding day, 1956
with Beatrice Kay.

Irene planting an olive tree on the Avenue of the Righteous Among the Nations at Yad Vashem Holocaust Memorial, 1982, Jerusalem, Israel.

The Gut sisters, 1984, Poland. Standing, from left to right: Władzia, Bronia, Marysia; seated from left to right: Irene and Janina.

Janina Opdyke Smith, on the Avenue of the Righteous Among the Nations next to her mothers' tree, 1987, Yad Vashem, Jerusalem, Israel.

Irene recieving an honorary Doctorate of Humane Letters at Haverford College, 1994, Haverford, Pennsylvania.

Irene with Herschl Morris, 1997, Tel Aviv, Israel.

Irene with Dr Mordechai Paldiel, Curator of Yad Vashem, on the grounds of the Memorial, 1997, Jerusalem, Israel.

Irene Gut Opdyke.

particular were determined to continue their old Christmas traditions.

The HKP party would include officers from all over the district; there would be a great deal of extra work, and Schulz warned me that everyone would have to help out with serving. So far, I had kept Janina from direct contact with the officers; I didn't want to bring my pretty young sister to their attention. But with the party as big as it would be, I knew I could not persuade Schulz to let me keep Janina off duty.

In the kitchen, we were busy for days ahead of time, preparing cakes and sweets and other delicacies. Without the new workers I had brought from the *Arbeitslager*, Roman and Sozia, I could not have managed to do everything that had to be done. They were newlyweds, a young couple full of hope and dreams in spite of the despair that surrounded them. Sozia sang all the time, and Roman would gaze at her with such love that it hurt to watch them.

At last, Christmas Eve arrived, and the hotel was filled to capacity with extra guests. Janina was almost giddy with excitement: we were going to a party, even if it was only as servants. She followed behind me, almost stepping on my heels, as we brought the first trays of hors d'oeuvres into the crowded dining room.

The place was a roar of voices and laughter that nearly drowned the music from the phonograph. Every man was in his finest uniform, bristling with medals and insignia, and the secretaries were dressed in the latest fashions from Berlin. Janina gazed around her, her eyes sparkling. 'Irenka, isn't it splendid?' she whispered.

'Good evening, Fräulein Gut,' came a voice from behind me.

I spun around to find Rokita ogling my sister.

'Sturmbannführer,' I said, making a slight curtsy.

Rokita could not take his eyes off Janina, who was blushing under his scrutiny. 'Who is this lovely creature?' he demanded.

Fear bolted through me and left my fingers prickling. I could feel a flush of anger between my shoulder blades.

'She is my sister,' I said.

Rokita shifted his gaze to me. 'Don't tell me she's been here all this time and you've been hiding her.'

I could hardly draw my breath. 'Please excuse us, Sturmbannführer. We have work to do.'

I took Janina's elbow and led her away through the crowd. 'He's a very powerful and dangerous man,' I hissed. 'It's not safe to have him interested in you.'

'But he's so handsome,' my sister marvelled.

'Don't be an idiot, Janka. I've told you what he does. Next time you see him, look at his ring – that will show you his real face.'

I shot a worried look back across the room. Rokita was whispering in the ear of a sluttish blond woman wearing a low-cut dress. As I watched, she reached up and stroked his cheek with one painted fingernail. I shuddered, and hustled Janina back into the kitchen.

Roman and Sozia were busy washing and drying champagne glasses; Schulz was arranging slices of bread around a bowl of Russian caviar. 'Irene, I ran into someone in the hallway a few minutes ago who wants to meet you,' Schulz said.

I picked up another tray of hors d'oeuvres. 'Me? Who could want to meet me?'

'A local girl. She's here as Rokita's date. She heard I had a Polish girl as an assistant, and she thought it would be fun to meet you. Maybe she wants to be friendly.'

'Probably she wants to show off that she's sleeping with the head of the SS,' I muttered, thinking of the vulgar-looking woman I had glimpsed with Rokita.

The door opened, letting in a burst of noise from the party. The woman picked her way across the tiled floor in her high heels, beaming a smile toward me that was all teeth. 'You must be Irene,' she began. 'My name is Natasha. I heard that—'

She broke off, gaping at Roman. He had backed up to the sink and was gripping it tightly, while Sozia sent a bewildered look from her husband to Natasha.

'Roman,' the blond woman said in Polish. 'So, I see they've put you to work in the kitchen.' She looked at Schulz and switched to German. 'Don't you think it's risky to put these Jews to work in a kitchen where food for officers is prepared? I will tell Sturmbannführer Rokita about this at once.'

Schulz took her by the arm and steered her back toward the dining room. '*Verzeihen Sie, mir, Fräulein. We have so much work to do.*'

He hustled her out, but not before she shot one last cold look at Roman. We all stared at him in dismay. 'Do you know her?' Janina asked.

'I knew her before the war,' Roman said, drawing a shaky hand across his upper lip. 'We were friends, but I suppose she wanted something else. She wanted – she was very jealous and tried to hurt me by spreading gossip and slanders. My family threatened to take her to court, and she swore she would get even with me.'

Sozia put her arms around her husband and laid her head against his shoulder. 'Don't worry, my love. We are already prisoners. She can't hurt us any worse.'

And yet the very next day, on Christmas, they did not report for work. Herschl Morris's brother, Hermann, and his wife were brought instead. Roman and Sozia had been taken away.

I wanted to scream when I heard the news. Beautiful Sozia with her black curls and her singing. Roman with his warm eyes. Natasha had carried out her revenge, and Rokita had been her instrument.

I imagine it this way: Roman and Sozia had been dangling from the edge of a cliff, but I had been holding on to their wrists. I had been holding on, I swear to God I had been holding on! – but they slipped out of my grasp anyway, and when I closed my eyes, I saw their faces as if they were falling away from me into darkness. My head roared with the sound of their falling.

I tried to pray, tried to remind myself of the promises that Jesus' birth had made to the world, but when I closed my eyes to whisper my prayers, I saw only Sozia and Roman, falling away. Natasha's revenge made Christmas a lie.

And Rokita, returning day after day to dine with Major Rügemer, kept asking about Janina. The major was a gentleman and knew what Rokita wanted. Rügemer – I think out of kindness to me – kept putting Rokita off. But Rokita was wily, pouring schnapps into the major's glass and urging him to drink. I shuddered to think what the major might agree to while drunk. Time was racing.

Shortly after Christmas, I asked to speak to Major

Rügemer in his office. He smiled when he saw me, and waved me to a seat.

'Fräulein Gut, how may I help you?' he asked.

'I want you to let my sister go back to Radom.'

The major's eyes looked very large behind his thick glasses. 'What are you saying?'

'Herr Major, I think you know. Sturmbannführer Rokita is like a spider creeping towards a fly. I must protect my sister. Please send her back to Radom. She is so young,' I added, and in spite of myself, tears welled up in my eyes.

'Now, now, Fräulein Gut,' the major said quickly. 'Don't cry. Don't worry. I'll let her go.'

'Oh, thank you—'

'But, Irene,' he continued, 'you must stay.'

I felt a snag on my happiness. He had called me Irene. He was making a condition for Janina's release. Somehow, the light seemed to have changed, and I saw myself differently. I saw myself being watched by Major Rügemer. I nodded slowly, seeing myself in this new way, a way I did not like, but must accept. 'Yes, Herr Major. I will stay until the end of the war.'

When I saw Rokita that night, removing his heavy winter coat in the vestibule, he beckoned me forward with a jerk of his chin. 'Your sister. I want her to wait on me tonight.'

'I'm so sorry, Sturmbannführer. We have just discovered she has tuberculosis. We are sending her away. It's very contagious.'

Rokita recoiled. He stared at me with something like disgust for a moment, then turned on his heel and entered the dining room without another word. He had stolen Roman and Sozia. But he would not get Janina.

But now, as 1943 began, my last link with my family was gone.

Puszcza Janówka

I had one consolation: Helen Weinbaum had moved to a farm outside Ternopol. We crossed paths in town on a bitter cold day, and quickly brought each other up to date as we huddled in the shelter of a boarded-up bookstall. Helen had learned that her husband, Henry, was Rokita's valet! As a sophisticated, cultured young man, Henry was indispensable to someone like Rokita: he knew perfectly how a gentleman should dress and entertain. Henry tended bar at the parties Rokita had at his headquarters and, like me, sent word of Rokita's plans to the ghetto when he was able. Now Helen and I promised to keep in touch if we could manage it.

It was impossible, at this time, not to know that the war was going badly for the Germans in the east. Since attacking Stalingrad in August, the Germans had been struggling without success to overwhelm the Russians. Stalin had decreed that the Red Army would not take another step backward, and the Germans and Russians had been fighting from building to building in Stalingrad for five months. The city was decimated, pounded to rubble by German shelling and scoured by blizzards howling up from the Black Sea, and still the Russians were not retreating. Thousands of German soldiers had been killed or captured. Our factory was on double shifts, speeding production of munitions until it seemed that the machinery would melt under its own heat. A Russian occupation would be no improvement for Poland, or for me personally. But for the sake of the Jews, I prayed nightly for the Russians to advance and crush Hitler's army.

As if fearful that they would run out of time, the Nazis began speeding up their *Aktions* against the Jews in the spring of 1943. Rokita and his Sturmbann made forays to 'thin' the ghetto and the *Arbeitslager* with increasing frequency.

'Many people are choosing to hide in the *puszcza*,' Herschl Morris told me one day in the laundry room. 'Better to live like wild beasts in the forest than wait for death in the ghetto. My brother and I have decided that we will go, too. We will take our wives and hide in the forest.'

I was examining the hiding place they had built behind the wall of shelving, and I looked at Herschl with some surprise. 'How will you live?'

He smiled wryly. 'As free men.'

'Not free,' Steiner broke in with a sour face. 'As hunted men.'

'We'll take our chances in Puszcza Janówka,' Herschl insisted. He turned to me. 'And Irene, you must help us to get there.'

I looked from Herschl to his wife and back again. 'Give me a few days,' I said, and then left the laundry room without further discussion.

I did not ask myself, Should I do this? But, How will I do this? Every step of my childhood had brought me to this crossroad; I must take the right path, or I would no longer be myself.

You must understand that I did not become a resistance fighter, a smuggler of Jews, a defier of the SS and the Nazis, all at once. One's first steps are always small: I had begun by hiding food under a fence. Now I was making plans to get a *dorożka*, a wagon, from the farm where Helen lived, and to transport in secret the Morris brothers and their wives ten kilometres from Ternopol, to the black-shadowed forest of Janówka.

But even my first feeble efforts to help the Jews back in the Radom ghetto could have brought me a bullet in the head; I knew I could only be killed once, and, as the saying went, I might as well be hanged for a sheep as for a lamb. The Nazis did not distinguish between leaving food under a fence and smuggling four people in a *dorożka*, and so I did not, either. Even so, I was thankful that Janina was gone, because what I was planning now could have put her in mortal danger, too.

I was now twenty-one years old, and I had been a fighter on and off for four years. Those four years should have been spent in school, or in falling in love and starting a family, or in working at a job, or in a hundred other ways. But that was not to be. For four years I had been in the middle of war, and I had different hopes and expectations now. I only wanted not to die in too much pain, and to foil the Germans as much as I could before I went.

On a morning late in May, Helen arrived with the wagon. I had already secured permission from Schulz to take the day off, and the Morrises had committed themselves to hiding by the roadside overnight. I did not ask how they would escape the *Arbeitslager*; if they could do it, they would. I would be on the road with the wagon. This *dorożka* had been rented from the farm with vodka and cigarettes I stole from the supply room. Abrupt, telegraphic flashes of surprise sparked in my mind as I climbed up onto the driving seat: trading in stolen goods, smuggling runaway Jews. It was almost unbelievable that I was the one doing these things.

I left Ternopol, going north toward the village of Janówka, begging the warm sun and the steady clop-clop of the horse's hooves to settle my nerves. I kept my gaze on the beast's bony rump moving in front of me, watching as the horse twitched at flies, tipping my ear to the whispery whisk of the long tail hairs which were flecked with bits of straw.

A kilometre or so outside Ternopol, the road narrowed as it went through a stand of birch trees. I heard a whistle, and then someone called my name. I pulled back on the reins, halting the *dorożka*. Ahead of me the road stretched empty until it rounded the corner of a potato field. A look over my shoulder showed the way was clear behind me. There was nothing to see but the dust from my wheels drifting sideways in the sunlight. I nodded, and the four Morrises slipped through the trees, clambering quickly into the bed of the *dorożka* and hiding themselves under the load of hay and bags of potatoes without speaking.

I clucked to the horse and we were off again. I had been stopped for less than a minute, and when I emerged from the copse of birch trees, no-one could have known that the *dorożka* now had four new occupants. I breathed deeply, willing myself to stay relaxed and calm. After a while, the spire of a church came into view, and we were soon rolling through the tiny village of Janówka. Chickens and geese scurried out of the road, scolding as we passed. At the church, an old priest was bent over, tending a rosebush. He looked up at me and smiled kindly.

I could not say why, but his smile gave me new courage. I turned my face back to the road, and it seemed that in no time, the dark edge of the forest came into view, like a curtain being pulled across a window. The road was silent but for the hiss of the rubber tyres over the dirt and the clopping of the horse's hooves. I suspected that I was being watched; we all knew by now that Puszcza Janówka held more than foxes and wild boar. It was filled with fugitives and partisans, the war's outlaws. The Germans did not dare to go there in small patrols.

The road became narrow, and the shadows of the pines made pockets of cold air that we travelled through. I heard a far-off birdcall, and then another, and all the while, the horse was twitching his ears one way and then another, as though trying to locate something or someone nearby. At last, I reined the horse in and turned on the bench seat.

'This seems as good a place as any,' I said.

The hay in the *dorożka* bed stirred, and one by one, the Morrises sat up, spitting out bits of dried grass and seeds and pulling hay from their hair. Herschl stood and helped his wife to her feet. Hermann was doing the same, and all four looked around them with a mixture of curiosity and trepidation.

'Our new home,' Herschl said gamely.

They hopped down, as I did. Each in solemn turn shook my hand, while I clutched the reins so tightly with my other hand that the leathers left marks across my palm. 'I'll bring supplies when I can,' I said, roughly clearing my throat.

They stepped in among the trees, their footsteps muffled by the thick layer of pine needles. I stood, watching them walk deeper and deeper into the forest. They stood out brightly in a patch of sunlight, and the next moment they were gone.

I went to the horse's head, leaning my cheek against his muzzle and mingling my breath with his; I was the one who needed calming, not the horse. After a moment, I took the bridle and led the horse around, the wagon wheels bumping up onto the mossy shoulder of the road.

The following Sunday, I took two more of my friends from the laundry room, Abram Klinger and David Rosen, to the same spot. I held back the tears that threatened to come as they climbed down. I felt like a bad mother who had taken her children to the forest and left them there. For several minutes I watched them thread their way among the tree trunks, and then the darkness of the *puszcza* swallowed them.

It was on my way back to Ternopol that day that I stopped at the church in Janówka. I wrapped the horse's reins around the gatepost of the picket fence and walked up to the vestibule. A bee zoomed past my nose on its way to a red rosebush just before I stepped into the little wooden church.

There were not many people. They were peasants, mostly, or so I judged by their dress and by their weather-beaten faces. They sat scattered like fallen leaves among the pews. The priest was speaking when I dipped my knee toward the altar and took a seat in the back.

I bowed my head and closed my eyes as though in

prayer, but truly, I was both exhausted and overexcited. I let the priest's gentle Ukrainian accent wrap around me like a tender hand, and at first I did not pay much attention to his words. But then I began listening, and I realized that he was encouraging his flock to resist the Nazis and to help the Jews.

'. . . and to remember those who are less fortunate than you,' he was reminding them in a quiet voice. 'Our Saviour commands that we not stain our hands with the blood of innocents. The righteous path is never an easy path, but at its end lies eternal love, eternal life.' Surely, he must know that the forest surrounding his parish was filled with hunted men. He was telling his parishioners to help them. What he was saying could well bring him punishment from the Germans.

I looked up and studied him with new interest. He was a very old man, bald and wrinkled, but he had an upright carriage and his voice had no quaver in it. I noticed him glance my way from time to time, and I thought his look was kind. The urge to talk with him was so great that I nearly jumped from the pew with impatience.

When the service was over, I lingered in the churchyard, admiring the roses, while the priest blessed the country folk, and one by one, or in small family groups, they took their leave of him and trudged down the road with their dogs trotting nose down behind them.

At last, he turned to me. 'Good morning,' he said. 'I am Father Joseph.'

I shook his hand, which was dry and papery, but strong. 'My name is Irena, Father. I was passing and your church is so pretty, I had to stop.'

'Perhaps God asked you to stop,' Father Joseph suggested.

I tried to smile, but I suddenly felt tears welling up in me. 'Perhaps.' I fingered the blossom of a rose, trying to order the thoughts that raced through my head like the bees diving into the flowers. I had wondered too many times in the last few years if God was watching me at all.

'Is this your *dorożka*?' the priest said, walking to the bony horse and stroking his nose.

I wiped my nose quickly, sniffing back my tears. 'Yes – at least, I borrowed it from a friend.'

'Making a delivery?' he asked. He turned his mild eyes to me, the eyes of a man who had seen everything and yet still loved people.

At once, my heart ached to confide in him, to lay my worries and responsibilities in someone else's lap. I joined him at the horse's head, rubbing its velvety nose as I spoke. 'I would like to tell you – I would like to tell you about something that happened to me, Father, when I was captured by the Russians.'

Father Joseph nodded, as if he already knew. But he bowed his head as if in the confessional, and touched my hand gently. So I told him. I told him everything that had happened to me, and all the lies I had told, all the deceits I had sworn to. The only thing I did not tell him was that I was helping Jews escape. It was too dangerous a secret to share.

When I was finished, I looked at him anxiously, waiting to hear the sort of sorrowful rebuke that so many priests specialized in. But Father Joseph only nodded again.

'Irena, this is a war. God knows your heart. And God

knows what you are doing with that *dorożka* today.'

We were silent for a moment, while the horse eased his weight from one sore hoof to another and gave a patient sigh.

'Thank you, Father Joseph,' I said at last.

'When you come through Janówka next time, stop and visit me.'

I had begun gathering the reins in my hand. I looked over my shoulder at him. 'Next time?'

Father Joseph made a small wave as he walked back towards the church. *'Do zobaczenia.'*

The Blows of the Axe

I had taken six people to the forest, and although they had disappeared, they were never far from my thoughts. When I could, I borrowed the *dorożka* from Helen's farm and drove to Janówka, where I left bundles of food. Sometimes, peering into the depths of the forest, I would hold myself very still, as though my friends could only become visible to me if I were very quiet, as though this were an enchanted forest and everyone in it was living under a sorcerer's curse. Sometimes, I thought I heard the far-off blows of an axe.

I would tip my head to the side, frowning, yearning to hear a familiar voice call my name, but the only calls were from cuckoos, who flickered in and out of shadow among the tall pine pillars. The heavy heat of June pressed down from above. The trees held their breath. I would leave my offerings at the base of a tree and back slowly away, turning only at the last minute to climb back into the *dorożka*. The bony horse knew the route perfectly well, now.

I did not always stop at the church to see Father Joseph. Occasionally, I was in too great a hurry, and had to be back to serve a meal. Or else I would see the old priest, with his straw gardening hat shielding his eyes from the sun, leaning on a pitchfork and talking with a neighbour. He knew what my trips to the *puszcza* meant. I was sure of it. I did not know if anyone else in the village noticed my comings and goings to the forest. In those days, people were either especially nosy, or they kept anxiously to themselves – but no-one ever seemed to recognize me or take notice

And to my surprise – and relief – no-one at HKP took much notice of my comings and goings. More officers had been arriving in ones and twos, and the place always seemed to be in some sort of upheaval. I could tell Major Rügemer was very distracted: because of Rokita's *Aktions*, the major never knew how many Jewish workers he'd have in the factory, and yet Berlin was demanding ever greater efficiency all the time. This was the sort of crazy and self-defeating policy that was typical of the Nazi leaders. They wanted to get rid of the Jews, but they wanted the factories to run nonstop to provide weaponry and ammunition for fighting the Russians and the Allies. Rokita was fulfilling one part of the policy, making it impossible for Rügemer to fulfill the other.

'More men from Berlin are arriving next week,' the major said over dinner one evening. 'This place will be bursting at the seams.'

'No doubt they are needed for the greater effort,' said a captain named Hess, wiping grease from his fat lips with the back of his hand.

Rügemer frowned into his wine. 'I think I'd like to get a place in town. Too many young men here for an old man like me. Does anyone know of a villa?'

'Take any one you like,' Rokita said airily. He waved his knife in a careless gesture that dripped gravy on the table-cloth. 'You need hardly ask permission of the locals.'

The major frowned again, obviously finding the SS

man's manners offensive. He pushed his plate away. I had been clearing the next table, but I quickly moved to the major's side.

'Finished, Herr Major?' I asked.

'*Danke schön*, Irene.'

There were five others at his table tonight, and once the major had pushed his plate away, the others seemed ready to let me clear. Four of the officers left the table to pour themselves drinks at the bar, leaving Rokita and Rügemer behind. I picked up plates still heavy with food, silently cursing these men for wasting so much.

'Well, what am I supposed to do now?' the major asked irritably.

'For a villa?' Rokita asked. The major shook his head, and Rokita shrugged. 'The Jews? If you're worried about your factory, don't be. We'll find substitute workers.'

The major hunched over his wineglass, gazing down into his own red reflection. 'It will take time, cause delays.'

'I regret that that cannot be helped, Major,' Rokita replied without sounding the least bit regretful. 'Listen, I'll tell you something, since you are my friend. You must know by now the Führer wants all the Jews exterminated. Once we finish with them, we'll eliminate the Poles and their tiresome Catholic church. Of course, the Aryan types, like Irene, we'll make good Germans out of them. You will have your workers. But we must cleanse this land once and for all. We're scheduled to finish with the Jews soon. By the end of July.'

I hoisted my heavy tray, my ears ringing. Every one of Rokita's words had been like the blow of an axe and my legs were shaking so badly that I was afraid they would buckle. Hitler wanted to exterminate all the Jews, and then kill the rest of my countrymen. In my heart, perhaps I had known it all along, but always I had looked away before I saw the whole truth. There was no hope for my friends as long as they were under Nazi control. No hope at all. Tears began welling up in my eyes, and it seemed to me that I saw the faces of my friends in the laundry room swimming before me – Ida, Lazar, Fanka, and the others. They were doomed. There was less than a month left to them.

Just before I reached the kitchen, my strength gave way, and the entire tray of dishes toppled to the floor. The crash was deafening, and every head turned my way. Through a blur of tears, I saw the major and Rokita looking at me.

'I – twisted my ankle,' I blurted out.

Schulz bustled out from the kitchen, exclaiming over the ruined dishes and scolding me not to cut myself on broken glass.

'I have to take care of this,' I mumbled, reaching for a shard. Tears dropped onto my hands. 'It's all up to me.'

'I'll help, Irene.'

I looked miserably into Schulz's face. Maybe he thought I was talking about the broken dishes. But I think he did not.

The major called me to his office the next day. When I arrived, he was standing at the window. I believe he was looking at the Nazi banner hanging from the flagpole.

'Yes, Herr Major. You wanted to see me?'

He did not turn from the window. 'Yes, Irene. I have some news for you. I have decided to take a villa in town, and I will need a housekeeper. I can't think of anyone better suited than you.'

The axe fell again. I stared at the back of his head with a sudden furious wish that the old man would die.

When I didn't answer him, Rügemer looked around. His eyes were owlish behind his glasses. 'Does that please you?'

I twisted my hands together. All I could think of was my friends in the laundry. I did not know how I would be able to help them if I moved out of HKP. The major was waiting for an answer.

'Oh, that is very good, Herr Major,' I forced myself to say. 'I'm very glad you think I can do the job.'

He gave me a strange smile that was partly a frown. 'I want you to do it,' he said somewhat petulantly.

'Yes, Herr Major.'

'The house needs some work, which I'd like you to oversee. Schulz can manage without you for a while. Then I'd like you to come back and train a new crew. We'll be getting in some locals – Ukrainians, I suppose.'

My heart lurched. 'What is wrong with the old crew? Did I not train them well enough?'

He turned his attention to some papers on his desk. 'It has nothing to do with you, Irene – oh, and my ulcer has been giving me trouble. Do you think you can prepare a special diet for my meals?'

Was I to spend the war coddling and cosseting an old German officer, then? I wanted to scream, or cry, or slap his face. But I was a Polish girl in a Nazi factory: I was not allowed my own emotions. I stood there, at a loss. I could not think fast enough to get out of this new job, could not find a way to stay at HKP, where I could do some good for my friends. I felt as though I were strangling on my own helplessness. 'Of course, Herr Major.'

Major Rügemer looked up at me and nodded. 'Thank you. That is all, Irene. Schulz will give you more details.'

Defeated, I returned to the kitchen. How could I have thought I had any power to help my friends? I was one girl against a giant force that could order me here or there at its whim – feed me rich stews in a warm kitchen or send me to work in a mine. One wild and useless idea after another passed through my mind, but there was no opportunity for daring escapes or rescues. I could see no way to do anything at all.

I avoided the laundry room that day I could not face my friends and tell them how futile their faith in me had been. I was so discouraged that I hardly even realized what Schulz was saying when he told me after lunch that we were going to see the new house.

'It needs work, I understand,' he said as he took off his big apron and hung it up. 'And there are two families in it at the moment. Ukrainians or Lithuanians – I don't know what they are. You'll have to explain things to them.'

I followed him outside, where a car was waiting for us. It was not a long drive, only a few long blocks, really; we could easily have walked the distance in fifteen or twenty minutes. From behind the car windows, I watched the summertime town glide past. Trees arched overhead, draping their shadows across our windshield. We turned on to a residential street, and the car stopped in front of a large, stuccoed villa set back from the sidewalk. Large gardens separated it on both sides from its neighbours; on the left, a driveway snaked back to an old carriage house.

'The major will certainly like this much better,' Schulz said as he hauled himself out of the car. He wiped his forehead with a handkerchief and squinted as he looked up at the windows of the house. 'So. We'll go in.'

We didn't knock. The outer glass door gave onto a little foyer, with another glass door closing it off from the front hall. Schulz turned the knob and strode in, calling out as he did. Even Schulz, who could be so sweet and fatherly, had that air of entitlement all Germans possessed in those days.

There were startled voices, and footsteps from different parts of the house. One by one, the people living there joined us in the hallway. I gave them the bad news as soon as they were assembled. One of the two families was Ukrainian, the other Polish. I explained to them that the major had commandeered the house, and that he was generously allowing them two weeks to move out. The looks they gave me as I spoke nearly broke my heart. I could guess what they must think of me – a Polish girl working for the enemy. But I have no choice! I wanted to tell them. You must understand this!

There was no argument from any of them. The house had been abandoned by its rightful owner, a wealthy Jewish architect, and these two families had moved in. Indeed, it was surprising that the Germans hadn't confiscated the house before this. Now the inevitable had happened: they had to leave.

Schulz and I began our tour of the house. It would serve the major very well, Schulz noted. On the first floor were a dining room, a parlour complete with piano and gramophone, and a library. Most of these rooms looked out onto the gardens and terraces and a little vine-covered gazebo.

Upstairs were several bedrooms and baths. The kitchen was vast, and a little room next to it would do for a bedroom for me. It was when I followed Schulz down to the basement that I felt the first stirrings of excitement.

'It's so elaborate down here!' I marvelled. 'A kitchenette, a bathroom, all these storage rooms. Were these servants' quarters?' I touched the light switch as I went through a door into the boiler room. The coal furnace, cold for the summer, loomed in a shadowy corner. Beside it lay a heap of coal. My gaze travelled upward to a coal chute. My heart began to beat more quickly as I went back out into the main room of the cellar. Several people could easily live down here.

'I think it will do very well, don't you?' Schulz asked, heading for the stairs.

I took a deep breath and let it out slowly. 'It will do perfectly.'

The Race

In the laundry room that afternoon, I described the house and its basement. Lazar Haller was nodding quickly as I spoke.

'I think I know which house you mean,' he said. 'It was built by a Jewish architect. There were rumours that he had a secret hiding place built in it somewhere.'

'Not that it did anyone any good, I'm sure,' Steiner said.

The others had dropped their work. In the silence that followed Steiner's remark, we could hear soap bubbles popping faintly in the washtub, and then the whine of a truck racing its engine across the compound.

Clara Bauer was pressing her hands together. Her cheeks were red. 'Maybe God meant it to do us some good. Do you think we could hide there?'

'I'm sure of it,' I said. 'Once the work is completed, I'll find a way to smuggle you all into it. It will be a week or two before the house is ready, though. That will give us time to plan.'

'We've been praying for something like this,' Ida said. 'God has heard us.'

We were all silent again. Perhaps we were all thinking what I was thinking – that God had been deaf to so many already. But now the opportunity was here; I did not intend to wait for a second one.

In the meantime, however, I could not forget that Rokita's fatal work was speeding up. In town, behind a small shrine to the Virgin Mary, I left a note for Helen to wait for me there in two days' time. We had agreed on this system for communicating; neither of us trusted the phone lines. When, at the end of the week, I returned to the shrine with a small offering of daisies, Helen was there, her head bent in prayer.

'We have to spread the word as quickly as we can,' I whispered as I knelt to place my flowers. 'The SS are going to wipe out the ghetto and ship everyone out of the *Arbeitslager* by the end of the month.'

'I think it must be because of the Russians,' Helen replied, crossing herself, her eyes on the Virgin's statue. 'If they begin to advance this way, the Germans will not want the Jews to be liberated.'

I folded my hands and closed my eyes as though praying. 'How can we spread the word? It will be hard to get all over town.'

'I can lend you my bicycle. Will that help?'

'Yes. Can you bring it tomorrow?'

'Yes. I'll warn people in the countryside as much as I can. I'll use the wagon.'

Footsteps passed behind us, and Helen crossed herself again and walked away. Neither of us had looked at the other through this conversation. I stayed a few more minutes, then returned to HKP.

As I passed the guardhouse and entered the compound, I saw Major Rügemer driving out. He waved when he saw me, and I stood watching his car turn the corner and go out of sight. I glanced at the guard. He was smirking at me.

'How do you like aged German sausage?' he asked me.

When I looked at him blankly, he gave me a broad, lascivious wink and jerked his hips forward, and my face instantly blazed. I scurried away, hearing his mocking laughter follow me. So, it was assumed that I was the major's mistress. I should have expected this, but still, I almost wept with humiliation. I rounded the corner of a building and leaned back against the brick wall to compose myself. The sun beat down on me, adding its heat to my flushed face. A pair of sparrows was taking a dust bath at the foot of the flagpole, throwing tiny sprays of grit and dirt up into the air. I watched them for a moment, letting my thoughts settle.

If I was assumed to be the major's girlfriend, then it would cause no comment to find me in his office. If I was assumed to be the major's girlfriend, there was no place at HKP that I could not go. I pushed myself away from the wall, almost wanting to thumb my nose at the guard back at the gate.

As if I had a perfectly natural reason to do so, I entered the factory and went to the major's office. It was empty. His last secretary had returned to Berlin only a week or two previously, and no-one had yet taken her place. I opened the right-hand drawer of the major's desk. In it, just as I remembered, were passes signed by both him and Rokita. I grabbed several and stuffed them in my apron pocket. They would come in handy, I was sure.

And they did. For the next several days, I rode around town on Helen's bicycle, and every time I passed a man or woman wearing the yellow star, I mumbled a quick warning: Hide, run away, the liquidation is coming soon. If a guard stopped me, I had only to flash one of my passes, smile sweetly, and push off on my bicycle in the sunshine. Getting away from HKP for my 'fresh air' was never hard. Schulz always gave me permission, never looking directly at me when he told me I could have an hour off. Sometimes I wanted to grab his arms and make him face me, and ask him to admit that he knew what I was doing. But I did not, and he did not. He waved me out, and never asked me how my rides were.

And I checked on the villa almost every day. The two families had been given some time to make other arrangements, and had until almost the end of the month, but I was anxious to hurry them along. Rokita's prolonged absences from HKP told me we were running out of time, and I often envisioned myself running a race with the Sturmbann-führer. I had to get the families out, the painters in, and my friends hidden before the race was over.

And then the fifteenth of July came. Rokita turned up at dinnertime, smiling and joking with the other officers, and drinking a toast to the Führer at the bar before taking a seat at Major Rügemer's table. The windows were open to the evening air, letting in the scent of grass and diesel fuel. Someone had turned on the gramophone, and at one of the tables, the men were celebrating the birth of a baby boy to an officer's wife back in Düsseldorf. The officer himself was already drunk, and making sloppy speeches to his friends. They howled with laughter and plied him with more wine, thumping him on the back and shoulders.

Rokita shook out his napkin and nodded toward the revellers. 'We'll all be celebrating, soon,' he announced to the major.

I was unloading a tray at the table, setting down the bread basket, a dish of beet salad, and some spaetzle. The major took a piece of bread and tore it apart absently, wincing as the laughter crescendoed.

'Why is that?' he asked Rokita, a bit tiredly.

Rokita grinned. 'Because, my dear major, by the twenty-second of this month, Ternopol will be *judenrein*. Won't that be wonderful?'

I picked up my tray and began walking away. My head was light, and my vision was closing in on me. I banged through the kitchen door and let the empty tray clang onto a table before throwing myself against the sink. I was afraid I would be sick. I retched, but nothing came up, only the sour sting of bile.

Schulz turned the water on and patted some onto my cheeks. 'Irene? What is it?'

I could not speak. I had the strangest sensation, as though I must shake myself out of my own skin, as though my body were a terrible burden that could not exist in the same space as my emotions. I wanted to sit down, but I was like a pillar of salt.

'Irene?'

I wiped my mouth with a shaking hand and reached for the towel he held out to me. For a moment, our eyes met, and then he turned away without asking again.

'Go get some fresh air,' he said quietly.

I stumbled out the back door. The last streaks of bloody colour were scratched against the sky. Across the compound, the door of the laundry room faced me like the door of a tomb.

* * *

The next morning was the sixteenth. The villa that was my friends' only hope was not ready; not only had it not been painted, it hadn't even been vacated yet. As I dressed I tried to decide if I should tell them what I knew, that we had only six days left. They would be devastated. There were six workers left in the laundry room: Ida and Lazar Haller, Clara and Thomas Bauer, Moses Steiner, and Fanka Silberman. Six of them, and six days to go. I sat for fifteen minutes on the edge of my bed, staring at a patch of sunlight on the bare floor, trying to know what I should do. In the end, I decided I must be honest. Perhaps together we could find our way to a solution.

'We'll never make it,' Steiner announced when I told them.

Fanka let out a small cry, which she bit off the moment it passed her lips, and Ida put her arms around the girl. 'Hush, Steiner. Shame on you for having no hope.'

'It's time to make a run for it,' Thomas Bauer said. 'Take our chances in the forest.'

'No, wait,' I pleaded. 'I don't know if I'll be able to take you, and it's too dangerous otherwise. Don't run. We can—' I paced the laundry room, feeling them watching me. 'Don't go back to the camp on the twenty-first. Stay here. I'll lock you all in for the night. By the next day, the house should be vacant and somehow—'

'Somehow, Irene?' Lazar asked heavily.

'Somehow! Somehow I'll get you into the villa!' I promised.

Clara glanced at her husband. Her face was deathly pale. 'Irene, you'll be caught. We'll all be caught. They'll take us

173

all. Let us go and take our chances on our own. At least you will be safe.'

I was growing frantic. I clutched at her. 'Please! Please don't run! I can do this!'

Steiner shook his head and turned away.

'We are in God's hands,' Lazar said. 'And in Irene's.' He managed to smile. To comfort me! Me! Their faith put me to shame. How could I presume to be their saviour?

And yet I had promised. I had to do it.

The next five days were a nightmare. Each time I went to the laundry room – and I had to, I had to continue my normal routine, in spite of the bitter urgency – I saw the question in my friends' eyes, and I had to reassure them that all would be well. Each time I left them I had to fight tears.

The twenty-first of July: Helen sent word that she was waiting for me at the guardhouse. I met her there and brought her back to my little bedroom, where she promptly broke down. Henry had been ordered to report back to the ghetto from Rokita's quarters at the end of the day.

'What will I do, Irene?' she groaned, banging her forehead with her closed fists as the tears spilled down her face. 'I can't hide him, there's no room! He'll be discovered!'

I slid close to her, and spoke into her ear, my skin crawling at the thought of German officers passing in the hall. 'Helen, try to stay calm. I have a house. By tomorrow evening, it will be safe for Henry to go there. He must hide tonight and tomorrow, and then when it is dark, he must go through the coal chute. Can you get to him to tell him?'

She turned to stare at me, her eyes blank. 'What? How did you—'

'Do you understand me?' I hissed.

Silently, she nodded her head. 'Yes.'

I whispered the address to her as I pulled her to her feet. 'Go now. Tell him.'

She nearly ran down the hall. I watched her go, and then prepared to spend the day pretending that nothing was wrong.

By late afternoon, I was jumping at every noise. I crammed some dirty towels into a laundry basket and crossed the compound. Jewish workers from the factory were being loaded into trucks to return to the *Arbeitslager*. One truck had already passed the gate and was shifting gears to turn onto the street. I went into the laundry room.

My six friends faced me. Lazar was standing by the wall of jerry-rigged shelves.

'Now,' I said.

Without a word, Thomas joined Lazar, and they began pulling away the two shelves that hid the opening. Ida pushed Fanka in before her, then crawled into the space. Clara followed, and then Steiner and Thomas. Beyond the door, we heard more trucks arriving. Lazar looked at me and then ducked to squirm his way in behind the shelves. I heard distant shouts as I replaced the two boards and arranged boxes and bottles on them. A casual glance would find nothing wrong, but the hiding place would never foil a determined search. For the time being, there was nothing more I could do. My hands shook slightly as I locked the door from the outside and stood watching the trucks – and the poor people climbing into them.

Two more trucks drove away. I tried to pray, but the words in my head did not fit together in the right order. I wanted to say 'Holy Father,' but I could not. I thought He must have gone far away, taking His name with Him.

Then, a flash of reflected light caught my eyes. I looked up and saw a window in the secretaries' wing of the hotel open outwards. A woman leaned over the sill, watching the trucks leave and tapping the ash off a cigarette. She was laughing at something – perhaps another woman in the room behind her had made a joke. Then she turned away. She hadn't a care in the world. I could happily have shot her.

I hurried to the dining room to begin setting the tables for dinner. Schulz was stocking the bar, and several of the officers were having drinks at a far table.

'Oh, Irene,' Schulz said when I joined him, 'I forgot to tell you. We won't be serving dinner tonight. There's a concert in town, and then a party. Nearly everyone from the plant is going.'

I found myself looking at the giant picture of Hitler on the far wall. 'Oh. I didn't know.'

One of the secretaries came in, the same woman I had seen just minutes before.

'Herr Schulz, a bottle of wine and some glasses, please, for me to take up to our room as we get dressed,' she said, ignoring me.

'Of course, Fräulein.'

While Schulz busied himself with a corkscrew, one of the younger officers strolled over. 'Getting yourselves all fancy for the SS boys, are you?'

She gave him a flirtatious look. 'Oh, we're expecting SS?'

'They'll be coming tomorrow to search for Jews. So many have gone missing in the last few days – there's probably one hiding under your bed right now. Shall I come take a look?'

She uttered a mock scream, and grabbed the wine bottle from Schulz's hand. 'No, thank you. I'll bash him over the head with this, if I find one!' she said, and flounced away.

The officers laughed, and Schulz managed a weak chuckle. 'Perhaps if you were SS, she would have said yes,' he offered.

A soldier stuck his head through the door. 'Herr Schulz. Your workers, have they gone yet? We're loading the last truck.'

Before Schulz could speak, I stepped forward. 'They went earlier. I've already locked up the laundry.'

The soldier glanced from me to Schulz and back again. 'Yes?'

I made myself nod. 'Yes. Would you like to take a look?'

'I'll check – that way I can be sure,' the soldier said uncertainly.

I made myself nod again, as automatic as a puppet. 'This way.'

Schulz followed. I could not look at him as we left the hotel and crossed the compound, but I began an almost hysterical chatter, hoping my voice would alert my friends to the danger.

'We really must complain about the soap they've been sending us from Berlin, Herr Schulz. I don't think it cleans very well. What do you suppose it's made of? All the whites seem very dingy to me. When I was a girl, we always laid our whites on the grass in the sunshine to get them extra white, and it made them smell so good, too, but of course, the ground here is too dirty—' I rattled my keys as I put them to the door. 'Here we are!'

I pushed the door open and hit the light switch, my heart cannonading in my chest. Schulz ushered the guard inside. The man took a couple of steps in and turned around. The room was not large, and there were no closets, only the wall of shelves. He shrugged and stepped outside. I jammed my key into the lock and secured the door again.

'They left earlier, as I told you,' I said.

The soldier shrugged again, and then made his way to the row of trucks. Schulz headed back to the kitchen without a word to me.

By six o'clock, most of the officers and secretaries had left, crowding themselves in laughing piles in the backseats of cars. Even Schulz had gone off to the festivities. Only two officers remained, groaning in their beds with head colds. The hotel, warm with the lingering summer heat, was filled with an unfamiliar silence. Soon, I did not know when, the SS teams would arrive. I had to think of a new hiding place for six people before then.

To keep myself busy, I went up to Major Rügemer's suite. I often tidied his rooms when he went down for drinks before dinner. If he had taken a bath, there would be damp towels to collect, and fresh towels to place on the rack. I opened the door to his bathroom.

A glimmering wash of light was coming through the pebbled-glass window and lighting the far wall, and because there was a leafy branch outside the window, the light dappled back and forth with the movement of the leaves. I stood looking at it, sinking for one moment into a place where there was no fear, no racing time, only the gentle sparkle like the light off a lake. Through an open window in the hall, I heard a dove murmuring.

Then I noticed, high on the wall above the toilet, a grating. I had never taken note of it before, but the play of light had drawn my eyes there. I tipped my head to the side, studying it. The grate in the wall was perhaps one yard square.

Curious, I stood on the toilet seat and threaded my fingers through the screen. It resisted slightly, but then came out as I tugged. With my hands on the ledge, I stood on tiptoe to look inside. It was a tunnel, an air duct perhaps, and it stretched backward into darkness. I fished in my apron pocket and found a loose button I had picked up off the laundry-room floor. When I tossed it in, it slid for several feet before hitting a wall. The duct was big enough for six people. It had to be. I would not find a better place than the commanding officer's bathroom.

Now I cursed the late-summer light that still spangled the wall. I would have to wait for darkness, and hope I could smuggle my friends in before the Germans returned from their party and the search teams arrived.

Aktion

Early in the evening, I took hot tea to the two sick officers, and fussed over them and urged them to take their medicine with liberal doses of brandy, which I had thoughtfully brought them from the bar. By nine-thirty, the hotel was mine.

I stepped from one shadow to another as I made my way across the compound to the laundry building. There was only a faint moon, and the plant was dark and silent. At the main gate, a guard stood facing the street with his back to the complex, whistling a dance tune. Making no noise, I unlocked the laundry room door and slipped inside. I did not turn on the light.

I scratched on the shelves, and then whispered the news about the air duct. Lazar and Thomas offered to go investigate it. In the darkness, I saw their shapes wriggling out from under the shelves. We paused at the door, then darted the thirty metres to the hotel entrance. Two lights burned by the front door at the opposite end of the hall from where we stood. Some of the partygoers would return by that door. I looked at Lazar and Thomas and pointed up the stairs, and then beckoned them to follow me to the third floor.

The grating was out in a matter of seconds, and Lazar boosted Thomas up into the opening. The duct creaked with Thomas' weight as he snaked his way inward on his elbows.

'Is there room for all?' Lazar asked.

Thomas jackknifed around and stuck his head back out. 'Yes, just barely. I think it will take our weight.'

'I'll get the others,' I whispered.

I dared bring only one at a time. One by one, I led them across the compound, our hearts banging with fear whenever we heard a noise from the street, or a branch tap against a window. Ida stumbled going up the last flight of stairs, but I hauled her up and we ran the last few yards to the major's bathroom.

'Use the toilet before you get in,' her husband warned her. 'We'll be up there for a long time.'

I hurried away to bring Steiner, the last. The six of them debated among themselves the best way to distribute themselves along the length of the duct. Certain spots seemed to creak more than others, and I brought pillows and blankets from my room to dampen the noise. Finally, I brought up food and some bottles of water – enough to last them through the following day.

'The major will probably be very drunk when he gets back, and he's hard of hearing anyway,' I said, peering into the darkened vent. 'But even so, don't allow yourselves to fall asleep – you might make some noise.'

'Don't worry – no-one could sleep in here,' Fanka said with a quavery laugh.

It was midnight when I replaced the grating and tiptoed downstairs. I was sweating, and my legs and hands quivered with nerves and adrenaline, but I had one last chore. I returned to the laundry room and tried to make the space behind the shelves look less like a hiding place and more like a closet: I put mops and a bucket inside, and a box of spare parts for the pressing machine. I didn't think it looked very convincing, but at least there was no trace that anyone had been there. At last, close to one o'clock, I staggered to my room and collapsed.

But I did not close my eyes. I lay staring up at the darkness, where my eyes showed me phantoms and fantasies – terrible visions called up from the last few years, and dreadful thoughts of what could happen to my friends. After an hour of that, I was nearly beside myself. Then I heard the sounds of people returning.

I tiptoed to my door and listened. Men's voices, women's voices – they were all drunk and clumsy, bumping into things and shushing each other with muffled screams of laughter, just as though they were teenagers sneaking back home from a kissing party. This went on for quite a while, and just when I thought everyone was settled there would be another burst of noise – snatch of song, a curse, a slamming door. The periods of quiet grew longer, the interruptions less frequent. At last, the hotel slept.

And finally, so did I.

I was awakened by gunfire and explosions. I sat bolt upright in bed, looking around in confusion. When I moved to the window and nudged aside the blackout curtain, I was greeted by the dull clap of detonation. Rokita's men were doing their work, the final *Aktion* in Ternopol. I could not keep the tears from coming. They spilled onto the front of my dress as I tied my apron around my waist.

Schulz was already in the kitchen when I arrived,

wide-eyed and shaking. He handed me a cup of coffee and put one arm across my shoulders. 'Irene, the pogrom will be over soon. You must compose yourself.'

Through the window, we could see smoke billowing up beyond the roof of the factory, from the direction of the ghetto. Behind us, the door opened and the major came in, pale and sick-looking.

'Schulz, something for a hangover,' he said, groping for a chair. He sat down, and with each explosion and burst of gunfire, his shoulders jerked. He was muttering to himself. 'Stupid, stupid war.'

In the dining room, the officers and secretaries were making their late appearance. Hardly anyone spoke, and when they did, it was with a sour, wincing irritableness. The entire German staff of HKP was hungover and in foul spirits. Beyond these walls, people were dying, but the officers and secretaries cared only that the noise hurt their heads, and that work would be hard enough today without disruptions from the SS. It was all I could do to serve those people breakfast, all the time knowing that my friends must be hearing the same terrible sounds I heard, and wondering about friends and relatives who had not escaped.

Finally, all the late arrivals had dragged themselves off to work. I was desperate to get to the major's suite and check on my friends. The moment the door shut behind the last straggler, I raced upstairs. The bathroom door was wide open, and I hurried inside, shutting it behind me. Just as I was about to open my mouth to speak, the door opened again.

I whirled around. A young SS trooper stood with his hand on the doorknob. He was turning pink with embarrassment at bursting in on me in the bathroom.

'Forgive me, Fräulein. I beg your pardon,' he stammered.

My entire body had gone icy cold. 'What are you doing here?'

'I – we have orde—' He pulled himself together before I did. 'What are *you* doing here?'

'I'm Major Rügemer's housekeeper, and I'm about to clean his suite. You are in the major's bathroom. Will you please excuse me?'

'Of course, Fräulein.'

Looking quite sheepish, he turned and let himself out. Obviously, he did not expect to find any Jews hiding in the major's bathroom. If he had taken even a moment to look around, he would have spotted the vent. And he would have seen the shadowy form of Ida Haller, sitting cross-legged behind the screen.

I closed and locked the door, and drew a shaky breath.

'Irene!' Ida whispered. 'You must turn us in. This is too dangerous for you.'

'No! Just wait. I'll let you have a break when I know the SS are gone. Don't do anything until I get back!'

I fumbled open the lock and slipped out the door, refusing to argue with them for their lives. I hurried back to my duties while the SS continued to search HKP. I was as conscious of their presence as a quail who knows a fox is nearby. My skin prickled with their movements around the hotel. By late morning, they had finished at the plant and gone away in their trucks, but detonations and gunfire from surrounding areas of Ternopol continued to break on the summer air all day.

As soon as the SS had left the factory complex, I had

snuck upstairs to give my friends a chance to stretch their legs and use the toilet. Then I ordered them into the vent again, ignoring their pleas to stop endangering my own life for theirs. I told them it was impossible, what they were suggesting, and that I would not hear of it. I shoved the screen back in place and left them still arguing with me in urgent whispers.

After lunch, I went to the villa on foot. The tenants were just leaving as I arrived; they cursed at me and called me a whore of the Germans. I stood silently aside to let them pass me; the lives of my friends were more important than my own wounded feelings. I prayed silently for them to hurry up, to leave, to turn the corner of the street and be gone, never to come back.

And then the house was *mine*. Perhaps the major thought it was to be his house, but I knew better. The house was mine, my treasure box, my sword, my hen house. I turned around and around in the front hall, owning the mouldings around the door frames, owning the chandelier over the staircase, owning the door to the basement.

I opened that door and went downstairs, taking the time to examine the space more thoroughly. As servants' quarters, the basement rooms were outfitted with everything necessary – two bedrooms, a kitchenette, a bathroom, closets. All the windows up by the ceiling, windows at ground level, were covered with dark cardboard for the *Verdunklung*, the black-outs. No-one could see into the basement from the outside. No light would show. I felt a surge of elation as I went into the furnace room and opened the coal chute. For a moment, as I stood clapping coal dust from my hands, I had a picture of my friends sliding down the chute like children in a playground. I even pictured myself, like a proud mother, catching them in my arms and setting them safely on the ground, while a blue sky embraced us from above.

Then the sunny picture faded, and I was left with one more question: how was I going to get them out of the major's bathroom and out of HKP?

I would need a key. The street entrance of the hotel was not guarded, and was well out of sight of the guardhouse at the main gate. But the door was always locked at night, for fear of sabotage or murder by the locals, I suppose, or of un-authorized late-night rendezvous. All through dinner preparations I tried to think of ways to get the major's keys, trying out first one then another story to explain why I needed them. In the end, though, I decided simply to steal the keys.

Everyone on staff was still suffering from the effects of their party the night before. The dining room was quiet during dinner. Voices were subdued, and barely a laugh rose above the sullen murmur. People tried to handle their forks and knives carefully to avoid clattering, and many officers and secretaries excused themselves early. There was little billiard playing or after-dinner drinking.

I went to the major's table, where he sat alone, nursing a glass of wine and looking down at his uneaten dinner.

'Can I get you anything, Herr Major?' I asked.

He looked up at me, his glasses catching the light in such a way as to obscure his eyes; he regarded me with a round, blank stare.

'I think perhaps I will take a glass of warm milk with me

to bed, Irene. And I'll take something to help me sleep. This has been a terrible day.'

I tried to keep the excitement out of my voice as I began clearing his dishes. 'Oh, I'm sorry to hear that, Herr Major. I'll be happy to bring some milk to your room right away.'

He pushed himself away from the table. 'Good. And to-morrow I will send some men to paint inside the house. If you could just watch over them, see that they do the job properly . . .'

'Of course.'

I practically hauled him to his feet and shoved him out of the dining room, so anxious was I to see him in bed and un-conscious. At the bottom of the staircase I left him and ran to the kitchen to heat the milk, and in five minutes I was knocking on his door.

Major Rügemer took the glass from the little tray and put a small white pill on his tongue. While he gulped down the milk I glanced at his dressing table. His keys were there.

He handed back the empty glass. 'Thank you, Irene. Good night.'

'Sleep well, Herr Major,' I said as he turned away.

'Hmm? What's that?'

I smiled and raised my voice. 'Good night, Herr Major!'

I left the door slightly ajar and hurried back downstairs. Now, for the second night in a row, I had to keep my vigil, waiting for the hotel to fall asleep. I sat on the edge of my bed, not daring to lie down while I waited, for in spite of my state of nervous anxiety, I was as weary as if I'd been juggling bricks all day. So I sat, staring out my open door into the hallway, listening to the sounds that came further and further apart. At last, the place was still. I kicked my shoes off and tiptoed up to the third floor.

At the door to the major's bedroom I stopped to listen; from within came a laboured snoring. I remembered the sensation of waiting in the wings offstage in high school, then taking a deep breath and walking out into the lights. There was the same fluttering in my stomach, the same twitch of muscles between my shoulder blades as I straightened my back. And so, I took a deep breath and went in.

The light from the hallway slanted in across the room and illuminated the dressing table. I gave a quick glance to the bed, which was in shadow. The major snored on. I closed my hand over the bulky set of keys to keep them from jingling, and then backed out, locking the door behind me. I don't know what I was thinking, for if the major had woken and tried to leave his room, he would have raised a commotion. But I could not have him walk into the bathroom until I'd got my friends out.

They were stiff, cramped, and tired. One at a time they lowered themselves from the air duct and stood rubbing their aching muscles. Fanka swung her arms in circles to get the blood moving, and Steiner's back let out a crack as he stretched himself.

'Let's hurry,' I said, opening the door to peek out. I waved them after me, and we went single file down the staircase as fast as their stiff legs would allow. They stood behind me, watching anxiously, while I found the right key from the ring in my hands; then I had the street door open, and they were stepping out into the fresh night air.

'You know the address,' I whispered. 'Go through the coal chute on the left side of the house and wait for me in the basement. I'll be over first thing in the morning. Go! Stay in the shadows, and God bless you.'

In a moment, they had disappeared into the darkness. I locked the door again, returned the keys to the major's room, and then threw myself onto my own bed, telling myself that they would make it. I did not allow myself to imagine otherwise.

Before I fell asleep, I felt a surge of triumph: Rokita thought Ternopol was *judenrein* tonight, that his *Aktions* had rid the city of Jews once and for all. But I had taken action myself. There were at least six Jews left in town. As long as I could help it, Ternopol would never be *judenrein*.

The Villa

The instant I was able to get away after breakfast, I walked to the villa as quickly as I could – quickly enough to put a stitch in my side and to break a sweat in the heat. I unlocked the door and burst inside, dreading the sound of painters bumping ladders against the furniture. But it was silent. I was in time – assuming that my friends were indeed waiting in the basement. The smell of cabbage and potatoes lingered in the air.

Almost fearing what I might find, I opened the basement door and clattered down the stairs, my shoes making a racket on the wooden steps. 'Hoo-ee! It's Irene!' I called out.

The first room was empty. Trying not to worry, I opened the door to the furnace room, praying to find my six friends – and Henry Weinbaum. The door creaked as it swung open into the gloom, and I called out again.

'It's Irene!'

There was an almost audible sigh of relief. One by one, figures emerged from the shadows: Ida, Lazar, Clara, Thomas, Fanka, Moses Steiner, and a young, handsome fellow I took to be Henry Weinbaum. I shook hands with them all silently, suddenly overcome with emotion. They were all there; they were safe and alive. And then, to my surprise, I found three strangers, who greeted me with an odd mixture of sheepishness and defiance.

'I'm Joseph Weiss,' the eldest of the three said. 'And this is Marian Wilner and Alex Rosen. Henry told us.'

For a moment I was at a loss. I had ten lives in my hands now! But there wasn't time for lengthy introductions. The soldiers from the plant were due any minute to start painting.

'Hurry, everyone,' I said. 'You'll have to stay in the attic until the house is painted. I'll check on you as often as I can. I don't need to tell you not to make any noise at all.'

This was met with grim nods all around. Then we made our way upstairs. The attic was musty; dust swirled in a shaft of light from the high window, and the air smelled of mouse droppings. 'Shoes off,' I said. 'Don't walk around unless you absolutely must.'

I locked them in just as trucks ground to a halt out on the street.

I kicked the basement door shut on my way to let in the soldiers, and then unlocked the front door.

'This way,' I said, stepping aside to usher them in with their painting equipment and drop cloths. When I glanced outside, I saw the major climbing out of a car.

'*Guten Tag*, Irene,' he called cheerily.

I bobbed my head. 'Herr Major.'

'This is splendid,' he said, rubbing his hands together as he came inside. 'I'll move in in a week or so, when all the painting and repairs are finished, but in the meantime, I'd like you to move in right away, so that you can oversee things. Don't worry about your duties at the hotel – if you can serve dinner, Schulz can manage without you the rest of the time.'

As he spoke, Major Rügemer strolled back and forth

across the hallway, glancing into the rooms and nodding his approval. His footsteps echoed off the walls, and he muttered, '*Ja, ja, ausgezeichnet,*' under his breath. Then, when another truckload of soldiers arrived, he went outside to meet them and show them around the garden. There were renovations to be made on the grounds, as well. I stood at the dining room window, watching him point out the gazebo and indicate which shrubs and trees should be removed and where new ones should be planted. Behind me, I could hear the painters beginning to shove furniture across the floors, exchanging jokes and commenting on the weather and the sour cabbagey smell left behind by the previous tenants. I heard one of them say '. . . the major's girlfriend.'

I gritted my teeth and prepared to spend the day keeping the soldiers away from the attic.

For the next few days, while the soldiers swarmed around the villa – painting, repairing, replanting – I contrived to smuggle food upstairs to the attic. I took fruit and cheese, cold tea, bread and nuts. I also took up two buckets to use for toilets. The attic was stuffy with the heat of summer, but we were reluctant to open the one window high on the wall. The fugitives had accustomed themselves to much more discomfort than this. They were willing to sit in the stifling heat, not speaking, just waiting. At night, when the workmen were gone and I had returned from the hotel, I was able to give my friends some minutes of liberty. They used the bathroom, stretched their legs, and bathed their sweating faces with cool water. But we did not turn on any lights, and we were still as silent as ghosts.

It wasn't long before the servants' quarters had been completely refurbished; I had seen to that. Telling the workmen that the major had ordered the work to be done from bottom to top, I directed them to start with the basement. Then, when it was finished, I waited until dark and triumphantly escorted my friends to their new quarters, fresh with the smell of sawdust and new paint instead of old cooking.

It was the start of a new way of life for all of us. Several of the men, being handy and intelligent, were able to rig up a warning system. A button was installed in the floor of the front entry foyer, under a faded rug. From it, a wire led to a light in the basement, which would flicker on and off when I stepped on the button. I kept the front door locked at all times, and when I went to see who might be knocking, I had ample opportunity to signal to the people in the basement. One flash would warn them to stand by for more news. Two flashes meant to be very careful, and constant flashing meant danger – hide immediately. We had also found the villa's rumoured hiding place: a tunnel led from behind the furnace to a bunker underneath the gazebo. If there was serious danger, everyone could instantly scramble into the hole and wait for me to give them the all clear. The cellar was kept clear of any signs of occupation. Once the men had killed all the rats living in the bunker under the gazebo, it could accommodate all ten people without too much discomfort.

There was food in plenty; Schulz kept the major's kitchen stocked with enough to feed a platoon, and once again, I could not help wondering if he had an inkling of what I was doing. I was also able to go to the *Warenhaus* whenever I needed to, for cigarettes, vodka, sugar, extra household goods, anything the major might conceivably need for entertaining in his new villa. Of course, the soldiers who ran the *Warenhaus* had no way of knowing that half of what I got there went directly into the basement, and I was certainly not going to tell them!

The basement was cool even in the intense summer heat; there was a bathroom, and newspapers, which I brought down after the major was finished with them. All in all, the residents of the basement enjoyed quite a luxurious hiding place.

And yet it almost fell apart when the major moved in at last.

'The basement is finished, isn't it?' he asked me when he arrived.

All the hairs on my arms prickled with alarm. 'Do you have some plans for it, Major?' I asked, keeping my voice from showing my fear.

He unbuttoned the top button of his tunic. 'I'm sure it will do very well for my orderly.'

I felt the blood drain from my face, and Major Rügemer looked at me in surprise. 'What is it?'

I did not have to fake the tears that sprang to my eyes. 'Please don't move him in here,' I pleaded. My mind raced with explanations. 'I never told you this, but at the beginning of the war, I was captured by Russian soldiers and – and I was—' My throat closed up.

The major frowned at me. 'You were what?'

'They attacked me, sir, in the way that men attack women.' I saw his face flush, and I hurried on, more confident. 'I cannot bear to have a young man living here. It brings back terrible memories for me. Please take pity on me.'

Major Rügemer dragged his handkerchief from his pocket and blew his nose hard, shaking his head in anger. 'War brings out the worst, the very worst in some people! Funny,' he went on, 'I always wondered why you didn't have a boyfriend, a pretty girl like you. I've never seen you flirt with the officers the way some other girls might do.'

'I can do all the work myself, Herr Major,' I pressed. 'You will not feel any lack.'

He put his hand on my shoulder. 'Of course, Irene. I wouldn't dream of making you unhappy.'

I smiled up at him. Sometimes it made me cringe inside, to get what I wanted by playing up my femininity. Yet I knew it was the one power I had, and I would have been a fool not to use it. For my pretty face, for the affection he felt for me, the major would let me have my way.

We quickly fell into a routine. Once he had moved in, Major Rügemer left for the factory every morning at eight-thirty. I rose at seven-thirty to start his breakfast, which he ate in the dining room. Often, he asked me to sit and have a cup of coffee to keep him company, and we would chat about nothing – about the nest of blackbirds in the gazebo, or the way the middle C on the parlour piano stuck, or what kind of pickles went best with pork. Sometimes, if he was planning to entertain, we would discuss a menu for cocktails or dinner or after-dinner drinks. He stirred his coffee all the time in an absent way, and the spoon would clink-clink-clink against the cup as we talked.

Once he left the house, I locked the front door and left the key in the lock; this would make it impossible for the major to unlock the door from the outside and come in unexpectedly. This was the time when my friends in the basement could begin their day, taking showers, brewing coffee, listening to BBC war news on the radio while I cleaned the house. They smoked cigarettes as they read the paper and compared the official reports from Berlin with what they heard on the BBC. I returned to the factory every evening to serve dinner, but I always went home before the major.

And when he did return at night and rang the doorbell (I told him I kept the door locked out of nervousness), I opened the door and let him into a house that gave no hint that there were people living in the basement. It almost made me laugh, sometimes, to think of the absurdity and irony of it. Under any other circumstances, it would have been hilarious, because this was the stuff of farce: upstairs, a deaf and snuffling codger, oblivious to the goings-on at his very feet, and below, the hunted stowaways, dining richly off the major's larder. They were like mice in a cheese shop guarded by a sleeping cat. Under the circumstances, however, I never did get all the way to laughter; a grim smile from time to time was all. This was, after all, a capital crime.

So our new life had begun. I got in touch with Helen when I could, and we both waited anxiously for the day when she could come to visit Henry. It came about a month after moving to the villa, when the major announced one evening that he would spend the next day in Lvov. I was thrilled: he would be gone from early morning until late at night. This was the chance I had been waiting for. It meant

Helen could visit her husband. It also meant I could go to Janówka and check on my other friends.

That night, I called the farm where Helen lived. Our conversation was in a code we had worked out long before.

'Will you be able to deliver eggs in the morning?' I asked.
'Half a dozen will be fine.'

'Six?' Helen repeated. 'Yes, I'll be there.'

And at six the next morning, with the major already on his way to Lvov, Helen drove up in the farm wagon. She was dressed in a long peasant smock and kerchief. I unlocked the door to let her in, and we quickly exchanged clothes. After I tied the kerchief around my head, I let her through the basement door, closing it behind her. I was sorry to miss their reunion, but I had to be on my way. I smiled as the sound of Henry's shout of joy reached me through the door, and the smile remained on my face as I locked the front door behind me and climbed up onto the dorożka.

I had brought food with me, and a small store of medical supplies. The horse's hooves clop-clopped on the pavement, and I kept the kerchief low over my forehead. There were few people out that early in the morning: an old woman sweeping the street with a worn-out, stubbly broom; a man pushing a wheelbarrow loaded with scrap lumber; another man carrying a ladder. Soon I was out in the country, surrounded by green fields and flowers, with swallows darting over the horse's nodding head in search of flies. I took a roundabout route toward Janówka, but it seemed to be no time before the spire of Father Joseph's little church came into view. I promised myself the reward of visiting with the priest on the way home if I had time, and then clucked the horse on, toward the forest.

As always, the stillness of the trees seemed to fall upon me like a mist. Pine needles muffled the horse's hoofbeats as I drove along the shaded road. I looked right and left as we went forward. To one side, a giant tree long since toppled by wind stretched away into the dimness, its dry roots clawing the air. On the other side, a patch of yellow flowers glowed in a spotlight of sun slanting through the trunks.

The horse started as two bearded men emerged from a thicket of blackberries. They approached the wagon, and my heart lifted when I recognized them: Abram Klinger and Hermann Morris.

'Irene!' they called out.

I scrambled down from the *dorożka* to embrace them. 'How on earth did you know I'd be coming today?' I asked, stepping back to look them over. They looked rough and dangerous: forest men.

'There are always people watching this road,' Abram told me. 'It was our good luck to see you.'

'Sometimes it is someone else's bad luck if we see *them*,' Hermann added.

Abram took the horse's bridle and led the wagon off the road, in among the trees. While the horse nosed about among the dry leaves for something green and sweet, we unloaded the *dorożka*. Abram and Hermann examined my delivery with the eyes of men accustomed to making do.

'Eggs; we'll be glad of those,' Abram said, touching one lightly with a dirty finger. He turned over a paper packet of white powder. 'Is this aspirin?'

'Yes. I thought you might have use for it,' I explained.

Hermann nodded. 'Oh, yes. Without doubt. Miriam has a bit of a cold, and this might help.'

'Are you all well?' I asked, looking anxiously from one to the other.

'Apart from Miriam, quite well, all things considered,' Abram replied. 'Summer is good to us. There are berries and mushrooms, and we set snares for rabbits. Sometimes we get fish from the streams.'

I had a flash of memories from my days living in the woods with the Polish army, and I shuddered. They might make light of their predicament; I knew how hard their lives had become. And although the land was rich with food now, fall would arrive all too soon, with winter shivering at its heels.

We exchanged news. They were amazed to hear that I was hiding their friends in the cellar of Major Rügemer's house. I tried to play up the farcical elements of the situation, and they allowed themselves a few laughs at the major's expense. They urged me to come deeper into the forest to see their camp, but I was worried about the time.

'Give my love to your wives,' I told them, backing the horse and *dorożka* out onto the road. 'I remember you all in my prayers. I'll come as often as I can.'

They kissed me again, and told me they would watch out for me every day. I climbed onto the wagon and gathered up the reins, and when I looked again, my friends had disappeared among the trees once more.

The ride home was uneventful. I stopped at the church in the village, but Father Joseph was away, giving last rites to a peasant who had contracted blood poisoning from an accident with his axe. I returned to Ternopol in the hazy light of afternoon, and drew up to the villa.

I sat looking at the door for a few moments, deep in my thoughts. Helen was with her husband; the Hallers and the Bauers had each other; even the Morrises, living as desperate refugees in the forest, had the comfort of family and friends.

And I had never felt so alone. A wave of pity swept over me, and my heart ached for my parents and my sisters. I had sent letters, but I had no idea if they made it to my family; I got none in return – none ever reached me. I tried to conjure up a picture of my childhood friends, of my family engaged in some pantomime game, or giggling as we stumbled over the lyrics to a half-forgotten song. But I only saw myself, as if from above, sitting alone on the seat of the *dorożka*, and it seemed to me as if the wagon behind stretched on forever, crowded with people, frightened people who depended on me to bring them safely home. I could not drop the reins. And there was no-one who could take them from me, not even for a moment.

The Forester's Cottage

And so the summer progressed. Our routine hardly varied, although from time to time the major had guests for dinner – my friends spent many uncomfortable evenings hiding in the bunker under the gazebo. One night, Major Rügemer threw a large party, and I had a scare when Rokita took a girl out to the gazebo. Ida had a cough, and I was afraid the SS man might hear her. I hastily arranged a plate of hors d'oeuvres and carried them out across the garden, calling out loudly enough for my friends to hear: 'Sturmbannführer Rokita? Would you like anything?' He came cursing out of the dark gazebo with his shirt untucked, and angrily sent me away. I hid a smile as I walked back to the house. The day after the party, my friends enjoyed all the leftovers and laughed loudly as they recounted the amorous scufflings they had heard over their heads.

In spite of the comings and goings of SS and Wehrmacht officers at the major's villa, I was confident. Perhaps too confident. I was appalled one day in late August when I heard a loud knocking on the front door. I looked around the kitchen, hastily scanning the place for evidence that any more than two people lived in the house. Fanka had been frosting a cake, but she dropped the icing bag and scooted down the stairs in a flash. The knocking grew louder.

I turned on the water, wet my hair, and hastily wrapped

it in a towel. Then I stuck the cake and the icing in a cabinet, checking around the kitchen to see that there were no tell-tale signs of extra people. When I finally went to the door, I looked out to see the eagle and death's-head insignia of an SS cap through the glass. I stepped quickly on the signal button and took my time unlocking the door.

'What's wrong with you? Are you deaf?' the officer demanded furiously. Another uniformed SS officer stood behind him.

'I'm sorry, I was washing my hair and did not hear you,' I replied, still stepping on the button. 'What is it?' I asked.

The men barged in and stood looking imperiously around the hallway. 'Whose house is this?' the first officer asked.

'Major Rügemer's. I am his housekeeper,' I replied as calmly as I could. I squeezed my knees together to keep them from trembling.

The officers exchanged a startled look, and strode out of the house as suddenly as they had entered. One got in a car and drove away, but the other remained outside. I locked the door and ran down to the cellar. Cigarette smoke lingered in the air, and newspapers were scattered on the floor. I cleaned up as well as I could, and spritzed perfume around to mask the smell of tobacco. When I was satisfied that no trace remained of my friends' occupation, I hastened upstairs again.

Not long afterward, car doors slammed in the street, and I peeked through the window to see Major Rügemer himself striding up to the front door, a look of fury on his face. The SS officers were right behind him. I let them in and stood aside, making my face a blank.

'The idea,' the major fumed. 'Jews hiding in *my* house! It's preposterous!'

The officers looked chagrined. 'As I said, we must have been given the wrong information, Herr Major. Please forget this misunderstanding.'

'Oh, no!' Major Rügemer flung his arms wide. 'Go ahead. Search the house. This is my housekeeper, a trusted servant. She will show you anything you want to see.'

Reluctantly, the officers looked into the parlour and kitchen. 'What's in here?' one asked in an uneasy voice. He was pointing at the cellar door.

I tried to play upon their discomfort. In fact, they were both so flustered I doubt they really looked at anything. 'There are servants' quarters downstairs,' I said haughtily. 'Would you like to see?'

'I suppose we had better . . .'

I had to fight back a wave of nausea as I unlocked the door and hit the light switch. 'We don't really use it much,' I said in a loud voice. Their footsteps thumped on the steps behind me as we descended. 'Just for storage, really.'

They stood at the base of the stairs and glanced around. 'Well, there's nothing to see,' one said, and turned back.

I heard the major's voice as we entered the hall again. He was shouting on the phone to Rokita. The two officers, looking even more nervous, offered Rügemer a quick salute and hurried out of the house.

When I had shut the door behind them, I felt myself go limp. A light switch dug into my spine as I sagged against the wall. Someone had informed the SS that there were Jews in the house. Someone knew, or suspected. I felt sick and dizzy. I could only pray that the major's presence was my security. The SS would think twice before following up a tip about this house again.

Unless the tip had been anonymous, someone was about to feel the wrath of the SS. I could not know who might have informed on me, but he or she was probably regretting it in a horrible way. I tried not to feel sorry for whoever it was; after all, that person had been trying to send my friends to certain death. But I could not help feeling a pang of guilt. I was responsible. I was responsible for so much.

Had I been careless? Sometimes, Ida and Clara and Fanka helped me with the housework, especially if the major had been entertaining the night before. We were always careful to keep the curtains drawn shut, but someone must have seen something. I tried to pray. What I prayed for was my mother.

But Mamusia was far away. I feared I would never have her to help me again.

Helen had told me, in one of our brief meetings, that there was a forester in the Janówka woods who might be sympathetic to our cause. He was rumoured to be a former member of the Polish army and part of the resistance. If this was true, he would be a good person for me to know. I must be prepared with a back-up plan in case of an emergency. At the earliest opportunity, I sought the man out.

I found the cottage several kilometres from the main road. I had taken the bicycle, and when I saw the wooden house between the trees, I dismounted and rolled the bike the last few yards. A tall, lanky man was on the roof, repairing the chimney.

'*Dzień dobry!*' I called out.

He wiped sweat from his forehead. '*Dzień dobry*,' he replied, gazing down at me.

'I'm looking for mushrooms. I work in town, but I have the day off and I thought I might take a walk in the woods.'

He nodded, and held out one hand as if to welcome me into the forest. 'Do you know which ones to pick?'

I smiled as I leaned my bicycle against a tree. 'I used to pick mushrooms all the time when I was young.'

'When you were young?' He let out a short laugh. 'Was that last week?'

'It feels like a century ago,' I replied, laughing too.

The forester climbed down the ladder propped against the house and came toward me. He had sandy blond hair, a drooping moustache that he chewed on while he spoke, and the kind of mournful eyes Janina would have called hound-dog eyes.

'You are right,' he said. 'These last years have been very long ones.'

While we had been talking, two small heads had appeared at the cottage window. I smiled and waved at the children. It suddenly occurred to me that I had not spoken with any children in months and months, and I longed to play with them.

'My bear cubs,' the forester said when he noticed them. 'Come, meet my family. And I should introduce myself. Zygmunt Pasiewski.'

'Irena Gutowna.'

He led me inside, where his wife was setting out lunch. As though it were the most natural thing in the world for a strange girl to walk in on her, Pani Pasiewska invited me to join them. Soon we were enjoying fresh brown bread and hard yellow cheese, stewed mushrooms, and a bowl of blackberries. The children chattered about a very large frog they had caught that morning but which had escaped from their bucket when they set it down to examine an owl's nest, and Pasiewski and his wife urged me to talk about myself.

Wanting to sound him out, I began to describe my days hiding out in the forest with the remnants of the Polish army in the first dreadful months of the invasion. We were talking in Polish, and as my own beautiful language filled my ears, I felt a wave of homesickness so strong that I had to stop and turn my face away for a moment.

Pasiewski put his glass of tea down with a thump on the table. 'My God, I know you, Irena. I was part of that group, too. I was in the village that night you were captured. We tried to find where you'd been taken, but you were gone.'

I stared at him. 'I had no idea that was you!' I gasped. 'I did not recognize you.'

He reached across the table and took my hands in his. 'How small the world is. I'm so grateful you are alive. I never expected to see you again in this world.'

At that, all my defenses gave way, and I put my head down and wept. There had been so many soldiers in that group, and I had been so dazed and terrified all the time that I had not really known any of them. I did not remember Pasiewski from before, but this man was a link to my past, even if it was a dreadful part of my past. It over-whelmed me.

So I knew that he had been a partisan then – but was he now? I did not dare tell him about the people I knew hiding in the woods, or about the people I was hiding in Ternopol, until I was more sure of him. In the meantime, however, it was sweet to feel I had friends. We talked about Poland, about places we had visited when we were young, songs we loved, our favourite foods – anything and everything about Poland that was safe to speak about. When I finally left the cottage at the end of the afternoon – without having picked a single mushroom! – I was happier than I had been since I said goodbye to Janina at the beginning of the year.

I would be back, I promised. I would be back as often as I could. And perhaps in time, I told myself, Pasiewski would be an ally in the dangerous job I was doing.

As fall progressed, I visited the Pasiewskis whenever I could. I told Major Rügemer that I had found a cousin living as a forester, and this made it easier for me to go to Janówka on my days off. Whenever I went, I brought chocolates for the children, vodka for Zygmunt, and precious white flour for his wife. Although we were friends, there was always a trace of reserve between us: when so much was at stake, it was hard to trust, no matter how much we wished to. We talked about the war, of course. In those days, it took first place in every conversation. He had heard that the Russians were beginning to advance towards the west, and that the Germans were growing anxious. The better I knew Zygmunt, the surer I was that he was involved with resistance fighters in the forest, but I did not ask. We were wary of each other's secrets. He did not ask why I sometimes came with an empty *dorożka* – empty after delivering supplies to my refugees. I did not ask where he had been when I sometimes visited the cottage to find Pani Pasiewska and the children on their own. We were close, but not close enough to trust other people's lives to one another.

One day in late October, as I was returning from the Pasiewskis' cottage, Abram Klinger whistled to me from behind a tree. I was elated at seeing him, as always, and followed him for about a kilometre through the trees to the foxhole where he and several others were living.

It was a crude shelter, only a deep hole they had dug and roofed with branches and a few scraps of lumber stolen from nearby farms.

'We need something better for a roof,' Hermann Morris explained, nudging at the roof with his shoe. 'Winter is coming . . .'

In emphasis, a cool breeze stirred the boughs over our heads. 'The Russians are advancing,' I said. 'Perhaps the war will be over before then.'

The women shuddered. 'The Russians. We pray to God they will not be worse.'

'I'll bring you what I can,' I promised. 'As soon as I can.'

As I drove back to Ternopol, I found myself echoing their prayers. I remembered the kindness of Miriam Meyer back in Svetlana. But I also remembered the cruelty of Dr Ksydzof and the Russian soldiers. I cursed both the Russians and the Germans: I wanted them all to return Poland to us.

But still, I had the responsibility of the people in my care.

I could not sit weeping over my lost country when their lives were so precarious. Especially when I returned to the villa that afternoon and Lazar Haller told me that Ida was pregnant.

The Coming Darkness

Everyone was despondent. What should have been joyful news was truly terrible. Clara, white-faced, took me aside and spoke in a low voice.

'It's been decided – we've all decided, including Ida and Lazar – that we must end this pregnancy. You'll have to get us some—'

'No!' I backed away from her, and stared at Ida and Lazar across the room. 'No, you must not think of it. Do not let them take another life!'

Ida had been crying, but she shook her head emphatically. 'Irene, it is impossible to consider having a baby here. The risk is too great.'

I backed away even more. 'No, let me think of something. The war will end soon – they say the Russians are coming. You've heard the reports.'

There was silence in the basement. Lazar took his wife's hand and stroked it silently. His chin trembled. The others looked at the floor, or at the table, or at the shadows in the corners. The furnace rumbled quietly in the other room.

'Please, wait a while longer,' I begged. 'Don't do this thing. Ida, please.'

Ida let out a deep breath. It seemed as if everyone had stopped breathing 'It is not my decision alone. We are all family now, and we must consider everyone.'

Lazar looked around, into the faces of his friends. One by one, they nodded. For a moment, I thought Lazar would still object. He was their leader, and must have suffered torments over the safety of his friends and the life of his child.

'We'll wait,' Lazar agreed at last. 'We'll trust in God.'

I went back upstairs, drained and heartsick. Already, night was closing in. I stood by the front door and looked out through the curtain, and saw the first flakes of snow circling through the coming darkness.

Schulz arrived in the morning, laden with rolls of tarpaper. 'For the windows,' he explained, letting them thump to the hall floor 'With the Russians advancing, we must be more thorough with the *Verdunklung* in case of bombing raids. Let's get these windows covered up.'

Some of the windows had had blackout curtains or drapes on them, but in the early days of the German advance into Russian territory, most had been removed. Now, however, the war was returning our way, and the threat of Russian planes had to be taken seriously. We spent three hours nailing the thick, oily paper over the windows, and when we were through, the villa looked wounded. The black windows made the rooms ugly and dark.

But there was one roll of tarpaper left over. We had finished up in the kitchen, and I eyed that last heavy roll as Schulz and I scrubbed the sticky residue from our hands. It would do perfectly to cover the foxhole in the woods: it was waterproof and could keep out the snow and rain.

'Schulz,' I said casually, 'where should I put this last roll?'

He glanced over his shoulder as he whisked a towel from the rack and began drying his hands. 'Oh, I'll take it back to the factory.'

'I was wondering if I could have it,' I asked. 'You know I have a cousin in the forest. I'm sure he could use it. And it's only one roll . . .'

Schulz gave a small shrug. 'I don't care. Sure, take it to your cousin.'

'*Danke schön*, Herr Schulz.'

There was a knock on the door, and I found Major Rügemer standing on the doorstep, smiling like a boy. 'Look what I've got!' Parked at the curb was a horse-drawn sleigh.

'Where did you find that?' I asked with a laugh.

'Being a major has some privileges,' he said. 'Come, let's go visit this cousin of yours.'

As often happened when the light was just so, his glasses caught the reflection and hid his eyes. I could not tell what he was thinking: was he testing me, to see if this cousin of mine really existed? There was no time to warn Pasiewski, but I could not say no.

'Let me get my coat,' I said. 'And Schulz said I could take this leftover tarpaper for my cousin's house.'

'Come, come. Hurry up then,' the major said impatiently. 'If we wait too long the snow will all be gone!'

It was a beautiful ride over the snowy countryside, but I could not enjoy it. I was too busy worrying that one of my friends in the forest might step out into view, or that something would go wrong when we reached the cottage. But luckily, Zygmunt was too experienced to be thrown off by a Nazi uniform, especially when he recognized me. He had been chopping wood when the sleigh came jingling into the clearing, but now rested the axe on his shoulder while he watched us.

'Cousin!' I called out before the sleigh halted. 'The first snowfall! Isn't it beautiful?'

'Beautiful indeed, Cousin,' he replied. He strode through the snow to meet us, taking off his gloves as he came. Steam rose from his hands into the frosty air.

'Cousin, this is Major Rügemer, my employer,' I said, introducing them in German. 'Zygmunt Pasiewski.'

'*Heil Hitler*,' Zygmunt said without a trace of irony. His German was heavily accented. 'Welcome.'

'Charming house,' the major said politely.

'Come in. Let me introduce my wife.'

I followed nervously behind, silently thanking Zygmunt for taking my cue. Pani Pasiewska greeted the major with a shy smile, and although she spoke only Polish, she offered tea and cake. As she showed Major Rügemer to the best chair, I hovered at the door.

'I'll just help my cousin unload the sleigh,' I said.

As soon as we were outside, I whispered to Zygmunt. 'Please don't ask what this is for, but I'd like you to keep this tarpaper for me. Please trust me.'

Zygmunt looked at me for a long moment. Then he smiled and nodded. 'Of course, Irena. I understand.'

'*Dziękuję* ' – thank you – I whispered as he hoisted the roll of paper onto his shoulder and headed to the barn.

We stayed for an hour or so, during which Pani Pasiewska hardly sat down for a moment. Country hospitality ordered that she offer her important guest the best of everything; and although the major begged her not to bother, she insisted on bringing out her precious best cups and laying a white cloth that had probably not been used since her wedding. The children, shy as fawns, hid behind the stairs the entire time and stared at the major's frightening uniform. Pasiewski and the major spoke of country matters, of the weather and the work that the forester did. Pani Pasiewska took down some wild-boar sausage that had been hung inside the chimney to cure in the smoke, and cut thick slices for us to eat with pickles; it was delicious, but I was too nervous to enjoy it. When at last the major rose to leave, I popped out of my chair with relief.

'I'll be back as soon as I can,' I said. 'Thank you so much.'

During the ride back, Major Rügemer chatted about the delights of country living, and reminisced about hiking trips he had taken in the German Alps and into the Black Forest. I scarcely made any replies, only thinking of what I would say to Pasiewski when I went back for the tarpaper.

Over the next few days, the weather turned mild again and the snow melted, turning the roads to mud. I could use neither the sleigh nor my bicycle, but when November brought another heavy snowfall, I was able to return to the forest. I found Zygmunt in the barn. His one cow was drowsing in her stall, chewing her cud as Zygmunt pitched hay to her. The strong, sweet smell of the cow and the fragrance of the hay filled the barn.

'So, you have something to tell me?' Pasiewski said, chewing on the ends of his moustache.

'Zygmunt,' I began. 'I need that paper for – for some people who are living in the forest.'

He shoved his pitchfork into a pile of hay. 'Irena, do you think I never guessed?'

I gulped.

'Come, come. There are many people hiding out in Janówka, and you are not the only one helping those poor souls. I was wondering when you would tell me.'

I felt such relief that I sat down hard onto the hay. 'I could say the same thing about you!' I said at last.

He grinned. 'Well, we're cousins. We should trust each other now. I'll bring you the tarpaper. Then you should be on your way.'

I led the way out to the sleigh, where the horse was blowing clouds of steam. Its mane and forelock were crusted with ice.

'Thank you, Zygmunt.'

'And you can rely on me. Remember that, Irena.'

'Bless you, Cousin.'

I hupped up the horse, and the runners cut a wide circle in the snow as the sleigh turned around. The wind buffeted my cheeks and found its way through the buttonholes of my coat until I was thoroughly frozen. The snow dampened the sound of the horse's steps and made the runners hiss as they sheared through the tracks. I finally pulled up along the side of the road nearest to where the dugout was, threw the reins over a branch, and hauled out the roll of tarpaper. Snow dusted over the tops of my boots as I began tramping through the woods, and before I had been walking five minutes, I heard a warning whistle. After that, I found myself with a familiar escort.

'Irene, thank you so much for coming,' Abram said as he took the tarpaper from me.

'That is to make a roof,' I explained, trudging behind him. 'How is everyone doing with this snow?'

'Miriam is very sick,' Abram said, his jaw set. 'Hermann is beside himself.'

My heart ached. 'How sick is she?'

He shrugged, making the roll of tarpaper nod up and down. 'I can't say, but Hermann thinks she might have pneumonia.'

I quickened my steps. When I arrived at the foxhole, I found Miriam feverish and coughing. Hermann Morris crouched at his wife's side, holding her hand. He looked at me with a stricken face.

'Irene . . .'

Miriam's shoulders quaked as she began to cough. It was bitter cold in their shelter. Even with my small experience of nursing, I could tell she was in very bad shape, possibly dying. I squinted up through the opening to see the light, which was fading quickly. Snow was beginning to fall again.

'Wrap her up in a blanket. I'm taking her with me,' I said.

Miriam opened her eyes and tried to focus on me. 'Irene?'

'I'll take you someplace warm, Miriam. You'll get better.'

'Hermann?' she asked weakly.

'Come, sweetheart,' he said, beginning to lift her. 'Abram, wrap the blanket tighter.'

Hermann struggled up out of the hole with his wife in his arms. Snow settled on Miriam's eyelashes, and she could not brush it away. Without speaking, we hiked back to the road, where the horse was stamping in the cold. Hermann bundled his wife into the back and drew the blanket over her. He looked stunned, as if he never expected to see her again.

'Can she walk at all?' I asked as I climbed into the sleigh. 'I can't carry her myself.'

'She'll walk.' Hermann stepped back, blinking back tears.

I had to trust that she could. The snow was falling faster, and it would be dark soon. I whipped up the horse, who needed no more urging to dash back to town. I prayed non-stop, prayed that Miriam would survive, prayed that the major would not be home when I arrived, prayed that I could smuggle this sick woman into the basement, prayed that the war would end before these people had to suffer any more. Snow flew out from the runners of the sleigh as we raced home, falling away into the darkness at the sides of the road.

The Punishment for
Helping a Jew

Luck was with me, and I added Miriam to my family in the basement – through the garden door and down the stairs, stumbling all the way, falling into the arms of an astonished group of friends. As the month progressed, the weather grew worse, and I shivered whenever I thought of the people living in the forest. All over occupied Poland – all over Europe; indeed, all over the world, where the war burned like brush fires in dozens of countries – people were living like hunted animals in the woods and mountains and marshes. It was late November 1943, and the Germans were prosecuting their terror as far as they could reach. Every day, we had news of reprisals, executions, deportations, massacres, invasions; the entire catalogue of crimes known to our kind was being carried out in the name of the Third Reich.

In Ternopol, we had our own examples, which were committed in public for the sake of instructing us, of demonstrating to us what our fates could so easily be. There was a deep cold pinching the countryside, and the winds whipped snow into high drifts on the weather side of the streets. I was coming home from the *Warenhaus* one Saturday afternoon, laden with soap and toilet paper,

218

taking a route I seldom used. It led through a square with a gallows in it, and ordinarily I went out of my way to avoid this sight, but the wind was piercing that day, and I only wanted to get to the villa as fast as I could and warm my hands around a cup of tea. I discovered a crowd blocking my way through the square. Black-coated SS men were ordering people to stay put and not leave until given permission. I craned to see over the hats and shawl-shrouded heads.

The crowd was being herded in a jostling cluster around the gallows. Someone shoved me from behind, and I stumbled forward among arms and shoulders and parcels of rationed bread and firewood. While we watched, a Polish couple carrying their two small children in their arms was forced up onto the platform, and behind them another couple with a toddler was prodded up at gunpoint. Even from a distance, the yellow stars on the coats of the second group showed plainly. There were nooses for all.

Their crimes were announced. The Jews were enemies of the Reich, and the Poles had been caught harbouring them. For the Jews, a sentence of death was the law. For the Poles, the punishment for helping a Jew was infamous: it, too, was a sentence of death. No trial. No mercy.

It took no time to hang them. No time at all. First these people were alive. Then they were dead. It seemed impossible that it could be such a simple matter to end their lives; and yet it was. We in the crowd stood mute, watching the bodies swing, watching the children's small feet dangle in the air. I had heard them choking. Now it was silent.

I might have fallen if the people around me were not pressing so close. When the shouts to clear the square rang out, everyone moved, and I somehow stumbled along with them. I cannot remember finding my way back to the villa, my limbs frozen with the cold and the brutality I had seen. Without thinking, I unlocked the door and shoved the key into my pocket with a shaking hand.

As always, I opened the cellar door, but turned away without speaking. In a few moments, Fanka and Clara came upstairs, and found me standing in the kitchen, staring at my packages.

'Irene! What is it? What's wrong?' Clara asked, immediately coming to my side.

'I – I don't feel well,' I whispered. I pressed my arms to my side to keep from shivering.

Fanka took my hands and rubbed them between hers. 'You're frozen through,' she scolded. 'What have you been doing?'

As if through a fog, I noticed a sound from the hallway, and before I could speak, the kitchen door swung open and the major came in.

There are these moments before calamity strikes – before the dropped crystal shatters on the floor, before the car's fender smashes against the racing dog, before the drunken man's hand strikes the child's face – when time stretches out and each second is wrapped in silence.

And then the world crashes.

Clara and Fanka and I stood facing Major Rügemer like statues, and the major stared at each of us in utter astonishment. His face began to tremble with emotion, but without a word, he turned on his heel and walked out. The kitchen door swung back and forth on its hinge. The library door slammed shut across the hall.

'Holy God,' Fanka whispered.

I banged through the kitchen door and ran across the hallway and into the library.

'Herr Major!' I cried out.

He stopped his pacing and whirled around at me. 'Irene! What in God's name have you done to me?' he shouted.

'They are innocent people!' I stumbled over my words in my panic, and began to cry. 'They've done nothing! How could I stand by and let them be killed? What else could I do? I have no place of my own to hide them, or I never would have brought them here! Do not turn them in, I beg you! Do not stain your hands with innocent blood – I know you are a good man! This war will soon be—'

'Enough,' he interrupted. He was red with fury – and fear. 'How could you deceive me, Irene? I trusted you. I gave you a home, I took you under my protection. I am a German officer! You have ruined me!'

'Punish me, Herr Major. I take all the blame – but let them escape!' I was sobbing, and I fell to the floor at his feet. 'I beg you. In God's holy name.'

He looked away, his chin trembling. 'Let me think. I must have time to think.'

I grabbed at his hand and kissed it, but he yanked it away from me and strode out of the room. As the front door slammed, I sank down with my face on the carpet, retching with sobs. 'Mamusia! Tatuś!' I choked. 'God help me!'

I had to drag myself to my feet and out of the library. I knew my friends in the cellar must be terrified. Groping like a blind woman, I tumbled open the cellar door and made my way down the stairs. The group faced me, ashen with fear. They were wearing their coats – even Miriam stood, huddled in a shawl and ready to flee.

'Don't leave the house,' I told them. 'Rokita's men will pick you up in a minute if you go out in daylight.' I began shoving them toward the furnace room, turning their stony bodies ahead of me.

'But Irene – this is madness,' Lazar said.

'Get into the bunker and wait for me – the major may not act right away. He doesn't know about this place. Wait for me three days. If I don't come back for you, get out through the coal chute at night and try to get to Janówka.'

I had to return to the factory that evening, as usual. As I walked along the frozen streets, I could only guess that I was walking to my death. Wild thoughts of escape thrashed in my head like birds trapped in a net, but my faint hope that the major would be merciful kept me from running to the forest then and there.

The major sat alone during dinner, drinking more than usual and refusing to look at me at all. Another officer came to speak to him at one point, but Major Rügemer waved him away without speaking. After my tears, I had become calm and resigned; I could only wait for whatever was in store for me. I returned to the villa immediately after dinner, and sat in the library with my hands folded carefully in my lap. A cold wind pressed against the house, and the blackout shades moved in the draft. The radiators clanked and hissed.

At last, the major came home. I stood up when I heard the door bang open. His footsteps across the tiles of the hall were shuffling and uneven. It was obvious that he was very drunk. When he opened the library door he stood swaying slightly, looking at me for a long time without speaking.

'Would you like some coffee, Herr Major?' I asked.

He kept staring at me. 'No.'

My uneasiness grew. I made a movement towards the door, but he stepped in front of me. 'Herr Major—'

He reeled toward me and grabbed my arms, pulling me toward himself. 'I'll keep your goddamned secret, Irene.'

His breath smelled of vodka and tobacco, and I cowered before him, my mind spinning. The loose skin of his throat had a gray stubble, and there was a tiny scab where he had nicked himself shaving. I knew what was coming, but I could not believe it. I could not believe it! His hands found the buttons of my blouse, and he began kissing my mouth and my throat, mumbling my name. I tried pushing away from him, but he held me tight.

'I've wanted you for so long, Irene. Do you think I'll keep your secret for nothing?'

I felt a fresh wave of panic. 'Major Rügemer, please—'

'I want you willingly, Irene. That is my price.'

Tears spilled over my cheeks. I was lost. He took my hand, and led me up the stairs.

Shame and humiliation flooded me the moment I opened my eyes the next morning and found myself in his bed. My whole body cringed, and I balled the edge of the sheet in my fists, groaning. The bathroom door opened. The major came in, buttoning his tunic.

He stood at the side of the bed looking down at me. He smiled uncertainly. 'Tell me it wasn't that bad,' he said in a small voice.

I couldn't answer. When he sat on the edge of the bed

and put his hand on my hip, it was all I could do not to fling myself away from him.

'I'll protect you, Irene. I love you; you must have realized that before now. I couldn't let any harm come to you.'

I forced myself to nod.

'And your friends will be safe here. I won't turn those women in, although I risk my own life. You understand that, don't you?'

I forced myself to nod again, and he got up heavily and left the room. A few moments later, the front door shut. Then I grabbed my clothes and raced downstairs in my bare feet. In my own bathroom, I cranked on the faucets of the tub. As the steam billowed up around me, I sat on the edge of the tub, pressing the heels of my hands against my eyes until stars burst inside my head. The tub filled. I sank into water so hot it made me cry, and my tears plinked into the water as I scrubbed myself. This was worse than rape.

I knew I had to bear this shame alone. I could never tell my friends how I had bought their safety. Their honour would never allow them to hold me to this bargain.

And as I dressed myself, I wondered how the major's honour would allow him to make such a bargain. I had always felt that behind the uniform was a decent man. I had never seen him do anything cruel or rash or give a reprimand where it wasn't deserved. But I had banked on his affection for me for too long, used him for too long. I could not be surprised now that it had come to this accounting.

When I finally went downstairs and called my friends in from the bunker under the gazebo, I was composed enough to give an entirely believable story. While they stamped their feet to warm up, I explained: the major had pitied them, and was sure the war would be over soon. He had seen only Fanka and Clara, and did not know how many people were actually down there. Stay put. Stay calm. I'll make it all right.

It was hard to tell if they believed me, but they had no choice. They trusted me, so they knew they were safe, but it obviously puzzled them. I got out of there as quickly as I could, so as not to face any of their questions. Then I put on my coat and wrapped a scarf around my head and shoulders, and went out.

The person I wanted to speak to was Father Joseph, but I couldn't get to the village at the edge of the forest that day. Instead, I found a church near Chopin Street, where a priest was saying mass for the first Sunday of Advent, the season of penitence. There were several people waiting to enter the confessional, and while I waited I whispered the Our Father under my breath. At last, my turn came, and I pulled the carved wooden door shut. Beyond the screen was the shadowy profile of the confessor.

I mumbled my way through the first few sins that came to my lips – stealing food, lying, wishing for the deaths of my enemies – and as the priest began to mutter, '*Te absolvo*,' I interrupted him.

'Father, there is something else,' I said, and when he nodded I drew a deep breath. 'Father, I have become the mistress of a German officer in order to preserve the lives of my Jewish friends.'

'My child, this is a mortal sin,' he said without hesitation.

I frowned, and leaned closer to the screen. 'But Father, if I don't do this, eleven people will lose their lives.'

'If you do this, it is your immortal soul that you will lose. They are Jews.'

There was a strange shifting in my head, as though a switch had been thrown. I pulled away from the screen, suddenly aware of the chill rising from the stone floor. From beyond the confessional, the murmuring chant of the celebrant at the altar was like the buzz of a fly beside my ear. There were dry coughs and shuffling footsteps from the congregants, and a piercing odour of wet wool and unwashed bodies.

I looked at the profile of the confessor again through the screen. 'Father, I cannot throw their lives away. Even for my own soul.'

'Then I cannot give you absolution.'

I shouldered open the door and burst out into the aisle of the church, walking quickly to put the confessional behind me. But I placed myself in God's hands all the same. God had saved my life so many times that I had to believe there was a reason. And I was sure I knew what that reason was: it was to save my friends' lives. The price I had to pay for that was nothing by comparison. I had not received consolation from the priest, but I had God's blessing. I was never more sure of anything.

And so as the Christmas season got under way, there began for me one of the strangest episodes of the whole war. Major Rügemer, as docile as a lamb now that he 'had' me, told me one evening when he came home that he saw no reason for 'those women' to stay cooped up in the basement.

'After all, I know they are there, so they may as well be

comfortable,' he declared as he stomped snow from his boots. 'Tell them they may come up. I don't mind.'

I gave him an astonished look, which he met with a smile. 'It's holiday time. We can all be cosy and company for each other.'

'But—'

'No-one can see,' the major pointed out, gesturing at the blackout shades. 'It's perfectly safe.'

'Very well,' I said, almost in a daze. I went to the cellar door and opened it. 'Clara! Fanka!'

They both appeared at the bottom of the staircase. 'Is he gone?' Fanka asked.

I glanced back over my shoulder. The major had gone into the library. 'He says you can come up and be comfortable any time he doesn't have company.'

Lazar and some of the other men crowded around the girls. 'Is he serious?' Thomas asked in a whisper.

I couldn't help laughing. 'Perfectly serious. Come on, girls. He wants to meet you. He really is very sweet.'

Fanka and Clara came up the stairs, both looking rather worried but a little excited, too. There was almost a holiday mood as we crossed the hall and knocked on the library door.

'*Komm!*'

Fanka looked pale, but she put a brave smile on her face. 'You're sure about him?'

'Positive. Let's go.'

I led the way, and stepped to one side to introduce the girls. 'Herr Major, this is Clara and Fanka.'

'*Guten Abend,*' he said.

Clara, being German, replied in kind, but Fanka looked a

question at me. Ordinarily, we all spoke some combination of Polish and Yiddish to one another, and Yiddish was close to German in many ways. But Fanka was clearly nervous about saying the wrong thing.

'He said good evening,' I told her. 'Just like it sounds.'

She smiled and made a slight curtsy. '*Dobry wieczór*,' she said in Polish.

'If you'd like them to help you with housework or anything of that kind, I don't mind,' the major continued. 'It wouldn't surprise me if they have been all along.'

I held my hands up and shrugged.

He laughed. 'Come, come. Let's all be friendly. I will not bite, I promise.'

Clara looked at me, shaking her head in amazement. 'Now I've seen everything,' she said.

Later that evening, when I waved good night to the girls from the top of the cellar stairs, I saw the men crowd around them to ask questions: we had been playing the piano and singing? And laughing? And had someone been dancing with the major? Fanka's and Clara's voices blended in with the others' as they related their story, and I shut the door on them, feeling safe for the first time in years.

But I was glad that they couldn't see the look on my face as I turned toward the stairs to the second floor. I went to bed – not in my own room, but in Major Rügemer's.

Into the Forest

The weather grew worse. My heart ached for my friends in the forest every time the wind howled around the chimney at night. I took them supplies whenever I could barter for the sleigh and get a day off. One day I was able to bring Hermann Morris back with me to join his wife, who was now much recovered. I had twelve people in my care, and I felt like a mother hen who cuddles a dozen chicks beneath her wings.

And to my great joy, a letter arrived for me from Janina at my aunt Helen's. It was the first letter I had received, and I was surprised to get it at all, but I was grateful for the news. Janina was going to join the rest of the family, and sent her love and prayers. I read the letter so many times I knew it by heart, but I still treasured the sight of my beloved sister's handwriting. I traced the words with my finger, picturing her in my imagination as she wrote to me. My heart was very full, for I had so many emotions to contend with: unceasing anxiety, continuing shame at my relationship with the major, relief that my friends were made safe by my bargain, loneliness for my family – sometimes it made me dizzy to name all the feelings that struggled to be foremost in my heart.

Nineteen forty-four arrived, and with it, renewed fighting on the Russian front. The battles were moving closer to our position all the time, and on some nights, when the town was bound up in the silence of deep cold, we could hear the faint, distant detonations of shelling to the east. People were beginning to leave Ternopol. Every night, in the officers' dining room at the factory, there was muted speculation about whether the factory would be closed. Everyone waited for news from Berlin. Hitler was rumoured to be acting unbalanced – paranoid and hysterical. The officers at HKP avoided looking at their picture of the Führer while they gossiped.

At the villa, Major Rügemer became increasingly distracted and preoccupied; to my relief, he was often too tired to ask me to share his bed. Over breakfast one morning in February, however, he suddenly set his coffee cup down with a crash and took my hand.

'Irene, I have bad news to tell you.'

'What is it?'

'Berlin sent word. A rumour reached them that I have a Polish girlfriend. I have to dismiss you.'

'But what about—' I could not help glancing at the door.

'Get rid of them! Irene, I can protect you, but even I have limits!' he said angrily. 'Of course, I'm very fond of the girls, but you must understand – they have to go.'

'Of course,' I said. It did not even occur to me to wonder what would happen to me. All I could think about was smuggling twelve people out of the house when the entire countryside was in a state of high alert.

'I have to go to Lvov today. I'll be gone for a few days,' the major continued as he rose to leave. 'I want them gone when I come back.'

'Yes, Herr Major.'

'We all have to leave Ternopol quite soon, in any case. You do realize that. The Russians . . .'

He picked up his dispatch case and left the house. While I cleaned up the kitchen, I thought through my options. At last, I went downstairs to deliver the news.

'Irene's coming down,' Wilner called out as he saw me on the stairs.

'Good morning, Irene,' Ida said. She eased herself into a chair, holding her belly: she was heavy with her growing baby.

'I need everyone to listen,' I began, waiting as the others, one by one, put aside their books and their mending and came to join me. I looked from one face to another, finding smiles, or looks of concern, or grave nods.

'The Russians are coming this way. I know you've heard the mortars. We've all heard them,' I said. 'It's time to move out. This is what I propose: I'll get the sleigh and take the men to the forest. As Hermann and Miriam can tell you, the dugout isn't very large. You'll have to make it much larger before it can accommodate so many people. We'll take shovels and picks, and as much building material as we can scavenge. As soon as you've made the dugout large enough, I'll take the women. Do you think this is a good plan?' I finished, sending a pleading look toward Lazar.

We all looked at Lazar. They always turned to him for leadership and advice, and we all breathed a sigh of relief when he nodded. 'It makes sense. The sooner the better, too. When can you get the sleigh?'

'I'll call right now,' I said, heading for the staircase. 'I'd like to go when it starts growing dark. Be ready this afternoon. Henry, you have the same build as the major. I want you to wear his extra coat and hat and drive with me.'

That evening, the eastern sky glowed like a sunrise, and flashes of mortar fire sparked along the horizon. I could feel the faintest of vibrations reach me through the snow-caked ground as I alighted from the sleigh in the side driveway and ran up to the door of the villa.

Henry Weinbaum stood in the foyer, examining his reflection in the mirror.

I saluted him. 'Herr Major.'

'Fräulein.' He clicked his heels together and bowed. In the major's uniform, he looked every bit the officer.

Together, we loaded shovels and other gardening tools and scrap lumber from the shed onto the floor of the sleigh, and draped heavy carriage blankets over them. Then, one at a time, we brought Lazar, Thomas, and Hermann up from the basement and covered them with blankets, too. Henry took the reins, and the horse lunged forward, kicking up great clods of snow.

With the Russians so close, the German army was in a state of alarm. We passed two patrols on our way to Janówka, but the silhouette of Henry's uniform showed clearly against the snowy landscape, and we were never stopped, even though it was after curfew. One soldier even saluted as we drove past! Obviously, they never suspected this 'officer' was smuggling Jews into the forest. Finally, with the sounds of explosions growing more frequent on the battle lines, we entered the forest. Hermann peeked out from under the blanket as we drew into the deeper gloom of the trees, and we stopped on his signal; the three men in the back slid out from under cover, dragging the tools and lumber with them.

For a moment, we watched them as they tramped in among the trees, carrying their unwieldy burdens under their arms. We soon lost sight of them. We turned the sleigh and returned to Ternopol. On the second trip, Wilner, Steiner, Rosen, and Weiss hid under the pile of blankets, and once again, Henry and I drove the ten kilometres or so to Janówka. The men carried the blankets with them to use for shelter, and then Henry shrugged out of the major's overcoat and laid the hat on the seat.

'God go with you,' Henry said. He began following the others into the forest, and then stopped and looked back, lifting his hand in a wave.

I waved back, and then he was gone. I made my way back to Ternopol alone, keeping a lookout for the roaming patrols. Once again, God was watching out for me, and I returned to the villa in safety.

A week later, with the major busy with the factory (and assuming that his house was now empty), I went back to the forest to check on the dugout. The men had been working hard, hacking and gouging at the frozen ground and chopping away at tree roots. Since I last saw it, the foxhole had been augmented with a ramshackle tin-bucket oven, whose leaky stovepipe filled the place with smoke. The shelter was almost ready, but despite the oven's warmth, the camp was wet and uncomfortable. I could not imagine bringing Ida there. She needed a better place to have her baby than a hole in the ground.

I stopped at the Pasiewskis'.

'Help me, Zygmunt,' I pleaded. 'I have a pregnant woman I have to get out of the house. She can't stay in the forest in her condition.'

We heard a distant boom of mortars. Zygmunt hitched his chair closer and spoke in a low voice, so that the children playing by the big stove would not hear. 'I have a place here in the cottage, between the walls. There is room for her and for another woman to help her, if she wants.'

My heart lifted. I put my hand on his arm. 'Thank you. When can I bring them?'

'Anytime. And what of yourself?' he went on. He nodded towards the east. 'Won't the Germans be retreating?'

I chewed my lip. 'I don't know – I haven't had time to think about it. But I have to go somewhere, in any case. The major has orders to kick me out.'

'You'll stay here,' Zygmunt said.

'But—'

'You're family, remember?' he went on. 'You must stay with us.'

I tried to speak but I found there was a lump in my throat. In spite of all the dreadful things I had witnessed, I had still met good, brave people during this terrible war.

'I'll be back in a day or so; we'll have to see what happens,' I said at last.

March 6, 1944, had been designated as the day for German personnel to pull out of Ternopol, leaving a rear guard to fight the Red Army. The Russians had been advancing steadily, and the boom and thunder of constant bombardments kept us on edge day and night. On the fifth of the month, with the major frantically overseeing the dismantling of the factory, I prepared to evacuate the women from the house.

'Helen is bringing the farm wagon,' I said. 'We're going to look like all the other refugees running away from the Russians. Pack anything at all – silverware, blankets, kitchen equipment, anything you might need in the forest.'

Clara, Ida, Fanka, and Miriam needed no further explanation. More systematic than looters, less careful than house movers, we stripped the villa of anything portable and useful. When Helen finally arrived with the *dorożka*, we began loading it with foodstuffs and household goods – bags of flour, linens and knives and featherbeds. The women wrapped themselves in shawls and scarves and, muffled head to foot like peasants, we joined the throng of wagons and trucks fleeing toward the west – toward Lvov, Drogobych, Przemyśl, anywhere away from the Russians.

No-one stopped us, because we looked like every other group of civilians evacuating the town. One old woman was prodding her skin-and-bones cow along with a sharp stick. A one-armed man carried a bulging sack over his shoulder. A priest herded a dozen orphans into the back of a truck. Horns honked, horses neighed, men and women shouted and cursed as the traffic slowed going over a bridge. How similar, and yet how different, it was from the evacuation from Radom in 1939! Now the frightened civilians were headed the other way, and they abandoned their town *with* the Germans. Soldiers were everywhere, of course, but they were too busy trying to manage the army's withdrawal to care about the local people. And the people – they wore expressions not of panic but of harried resentment. After so many years of war, they expected nothing less than chaos. They only wanted to get out of the way and preserve what little they had left. We stayed with the

235

convoy of bitter refugees until the road to Janówka veered right.

At last, we let Clara and Miriam out to join the others in the forest. Miriam recognized where we were and led Clara into the trees. We drove the last few kilometres to Zygmunt Pasiewski's. Fanka helped Ida inside while Helen and I began unloading the *dorożka* and stashing the food and equipment in the barn.

'I'll come back to see you as soon as I can,' Helen said, kissing me goodbye. 'Let me take the *dorożka* and the horse – we may need them. I'm not leaving Janówka as long as Henry is here.'

She climbed up onto the seat. Without another word, she slapped the reins on the horse's rump, and she was gone.

I knew I would never see Helen again. For a moment, I was alone in the clearing outside the Pasiewski cottage. Alone. In the distance, there was a dull thud of artillery, but here all was quiet. The cold air pressed around me, making the silence heavier. Overhead, crows were flying west. I followed them with my eyes until they passed beyond the trees.

Then I went into the house, almost in a daze. I had no idea where the war would carry me now. But I knew this: the Germans were retreating. Their lock on this part of Poland was broken, and my friends were free. I had brought them out alive.

'You are like Moses,' Zygmunt said to me.

'No, no.' I stared at my hands. They were cold, and I rubbed them together slowly, as if I had never seen them before. Shouldn't I have been happy? But I was oddly de-jected, because my great and righteous undertaking was finished. I knew Moses did not join the Israelites in Canaan. God brought Moses to Mount Pisgah, and let him look out at the Promised Land; but then, as God had ordained, Moses died. If I was like Moses, I would not live in free Poland.

What did God ordain for me?

Major Rügemer came for me a week later, with Rokita in the car.

'*Matka Boska!*' Zygmunt swore, looking out the window at the sound of the engine. 'There's an SS officer with your major.'

I dropped the bread I was cutting and joined Zygmunt at the window. The major was striding towards the cottage through the patches of mud and snow in the yard, tugging at the visor of his hat.

I threw a shawl around my shoulders and met him outside. From Ternopol came the sound of explosions. The bombardment had been growing louder all day.

'Herr Major!'

'Get your things, Irene. We're leaving.'

'Are the Russians advancing?' I asked. I could see Rokita in the car, drumming his fingers on the steering wheel. Behind me, the cottage door opened and Zygmunt came out, a strong and reassuring presence.

Major Rügemer nodded curtly at him. 'Our Panzer units will soon mount a counter-offensive,' he said to me. 'For now, we are moving to Kielce. Hurry up, Irene. You're coming with me.'

I turned away quickly to hide the tears that were flooding my eyes. If I refused to go – but Kielce was close to

Radom, close to Kraków. Closer to my family. I fumbled open the door and went inside to pack.

Zygmunt followed me and shut the door, leaving the major outside. 'Irenka, listen to me,' he said quickly. 'When you get to Kielce, run away from him. Ask someone for directions to Owocowa Street. Find the home of my brother-in-law, Marek Ridel, and ask for Mercedes-Benz.'

'What?' Baffled, I wiped away my tears with the palm of my hand.

'You can join the partisans – they need people like you.'

My hand froze on my face. 'The partisans?'

I could remain an outlaw. In an instant, I saw that this was what I had been waiting for. I had been living as a resistance fighter for so long, I could no longer imagine anything else. I would continue to fight. That was my life. That was the life I wanted to lead, struggling against the enemies of Poland. 'Revenge is mine,' said God – but I had many scores to settle with the Germans and the Soviets.

'Mercedes-Benz,' I repeated. 'Marek Ridel, Owocowa Street. Bless you, Zygmunt. Take care of my friends. *Do widzenia.*'

Twenty minutes later, I was hidden under a blanket in the back of the major's car, racing westward, away from the advancing Red Army and their crashing artillery.

For two days, our convoy of cars and trucks bumped and skidded west across the Ukraine. Major Rügemer and Rokita insisted I stay hidden, to avoid questions or confrontations by patrols; it was probably illegal for them to take a Polish civilian with them, and I marvelled that the major would risk so much for me, or that Rokita would go along. Huddled under a blanket that smelled of camphor and sweat, I repeatedly banged my head or bit my tongue as we jolted over the rough, war-scarred roads. For all I knew, we could have been driving back and forth along one stretch of road: I saw nothing of our journey. On the floor under the blanket, the road noise and the roar of the engine made it impossible for me to hear what few words passed between the major and Rokita, but it did not matter to me what their conversation was. I had my own plans to make.

I rehearsed lines that might prove useful for escaping from them in Kielce. I had deceived and outwitted them for so long, I was sure I could find a way to elude them now. For the first time in years, I had no-one's safety but mine to consider, and my thoughts flew ahead toward the Kielce partisans on eagles' wings.

In the late afternoon of the second day, Rokita left us to rejoin his SS unit, and the major took over the driving. My stomach was growling like a badger by the time the car stopped and the major told me I could come out.

I pushed the blanket back and sat up, smoothing my hair as it flew up around my head from static electricity. It was dark. I peered out the window as Major Rügemer opened his door. We were outside a hotel. 'Is this Kielce?'

'Yes. Come, Irene. I'll get you a room.'

Battered and sore from my ride on the floor, I pulled myself out of the car and stretched. Two dim lights glowed at the hotel entrance. I stumbled inside. The major was speaking with the clerk, who eyed me suspiciously as he slid a brass key over the front desk. Major Rügemer took the key and led the way upstairs. The narrow staircase smelled of beer and cigar smoke and urine.

'I have to report to my superiors, but I'll come back for

you tomorrow,' the major said as he opened the door. 'Try to get some rest.'

I edged past him into the room. He was leaving me there. I could hardly believe my good fortune.

'Is this all right with you?' he asked.

'Fine. Thank you,' I whispered. I turned to look at him. He was haggard. Anxiety had drawn deep lines from the corners of his mouth, and one of his eyelids was twitching from fatigue. In spite of everything, I felt grateful to him; he had helped me save many lives. I was already forgiving him for what he had put me through. I put a hand on his arm and kissed him on the cheek. 'Thank you,' I repeated.

He smiled wanly. 'Good night, then.'

'Goodbye.'

He paused for a moment at the door to look at me. Then he was gone.

part three

Where Could I Come to Rest?

To Fight

I slept heavily, exhausted by our flight from Ternopol, but as soon as I awoke the next day, I washed and dressed and left my room. I did not dare linger. Outside, patches of old snow lay heaped against the shady side of the buildings, speckled with soot and horse manure. I picked my way along the wet sidewalk, hugging my coat around me. When I caught sight of an old lady carrying a dented fuel can, I crossed the street to speak to her.

'Owocowa Street?' I asked. 'How do I get there?'

She set the can down, squinting against the pale sunshine. 'Follow this street until you reach the square. Then take a left until you come to Our Lady Church. Owocowa is in that neighborhood. Someone can point it out to you.'

'*Dziękuję.*' Thanks.

I kept my head down as I hurried toward the square. German military vehicles roared past, spraying mud and slush onto the sidewalks. I had no papers to show, and if I had been stopped, I would have had some tricky explaining to do. But after asking for directions one more time, I finally found myself on Owocowa Street. A boy throwing rocks into a puddle pointed out the Ridels' house. I straightened my coat and dress, and then my shoulders, and took a deep breath. I knocked.

A middle-aged woman with blond braids coiled on her

head and Zygmunt's mournful eyes answered the door, opening it only a crack while she peered out at me. 'Yes?'

'Pani Ridela? I'm here about a Mercedes-Benz,' I said.

She looked so startled that I began to wonder if I had made a mistake. Heat washed up my throat and cheeks. 'I came from Janówka. Pasiewski sent me,' I stammered.

At that, she flung open the door and pulled me inside. 'Come in. Come in. I thought at first you were German. How is my brother Zygmunt?'

'I left him two – no, three days ago,' I began, unwrapping the scarf around my neck. 'He and his family were fine then. My name is Irena Gutowna.'

Pani Ridela led me through the house and into the kitchen at the back, where a kettle boiled on the stove. 'Tea?' she asked, picking up a chipped pottery teapot. 'We've already used these leaves several times, I'm afraid, but we can still brew a little colour from them.'

For years now, I had been accustomed to having all the food I wanted, with the German *Warenhaus* at my disposal. And the Pasiewskis lived fairly well, with the bountiful forest as their larder. I had nearly forgotten how town-dwelling Poles had been scraping by – a potato for dinner, no meat, tea the colour of straw.

While she poured water onto the tired leaves and swirled the pot, Pani Ridela talked about her brother, whom she had not seen in years. 'I heard a rumour just this morning that the whole Ternopol area has been "liberated" by the Soviets.'

I sank back in my chair. 'Thank goodness. That's a relief.'

The woman shot a strange look at me. 'Are you a Communist?'

'Me? Not at all. I hate the Soviets,' I replied hotly. 'But it means that – well, that some people I took care of are out of danger from the Germans.'

Pani Ridela poured out the tea. 'Jews?'

I nodded wearily, happy for the chance to tell my story. Perhaps it was foolish of me to be so trusting, but she was connected to the partisans; I felt I could be honest. I gave her a summary of what I had done for the past two years, while we sipped our tea – hot water, in all honesty – and the neighbourhood noises sounded beyond the walls: barking dogs, a child calling its mother, someone hammering on metal, car tyres hissing through slush. These background noises played like the soundtrack to a movie while I spoke; in my mind they became the shouted orders of the Gestapo, the wails of frightened prisoners, the relentless clanging of machinery in the ammunition factory, the whisper of sleigh runners across frozen fields. While I spoke, Pani Ridela gazed into her teacup, as though she saw this movie projected onto the shining surface of the water.

The kitchen door opened, and a middle-aged man with blond hair going white came in.

'My husband, Marek Ridel,' Pani Ridela said. 'This is Irena Gutowna. She came to talk about the Mercedes-Benz.'

'*Dzień dobry*,' he said, nodding.

'*Dzień dobry*, Pan Ridel.'

He regarded me for a moment, then looked at his wife. I saw her give him a slight nod.

Marek Ridel excused himself and left the kitchen. His wife turned the conversation to Poland, and what our country's fate would be with the Soviets, rather than the Germans, in control. We talked at length, as the patch of sunlight from the window moved across the brown linoleum floor. It seemed I had known her forever, and I found myself pouring out my heart to her, tearfully describing my sister Janina's voice, my mamusia's pierogis, the dusky, sweet smell of my father's pipe.

'This is beautiful,' I murmured, reaching out to touch the embroidery on Pani Ridela's apron. 'My mother had one like this.'

'My mother gave me this one,' the older woman said. 'It has become so threadbare, but I treasure it.'

'I have nothing of my mother's. Nothing of my family's.' Pani Ridela covered my hand with hers, and I bent my head. I saw myself reflected on the back of my teaspoon; my image was distorted. I could not even find memories of my family in my own face. I had lost my family in order to care for my friends. And now that I was separated from even them, I was truly alone.

Then Janek arrived.

The door opened, and Marek Ridel entered the kitchen again, followed by a much younger man. 'My son, Janek,' Pan Ridel announced.

'I understand you're looking for me,' Janek said.

I lost the power of speech for an instant. One moment, I had been utterly alone. The next moment, there was Janek.

'I'm Mercedes-Benz,' he said, taking a seat across from me. 'Welcome.'

Love at first sight is a girl's dream. By March of 1944 I was almost twenty-two years old; I had long since stopped thinking of myself as a girl – and I had no faith in dreams. But suddenly, every sweet song I had ever heard made perfect sense to me. I loved Janek the way a priest loves God: without question. I followed him to the forest outside Kielce, where his group of partisans was. I followed him without question, and joined the partisans without question. I did it for Poland, yes. And I did it for me, because I had sworn to keep fighting the enemy. But even more, I did it for Janek.

They gave me small jobs to begin with, to test my nerve and my loyalty. I tucked messages into the thick bun of hair at the back of my head and carried them between the partisans and their spies who worked for the Germans. Sometimes I carried packages of money, smuggled in from England to be used for guns or sent further up the line to another group.

I never understood exactly where orders came from. I was never told more than I needed to know, and I did not urge Janek to tell me. It did seem to me that our partisan cell made its own plans and decisions, although we co-ordinated some of our efforts with other groups around the countryside. Mostly, however, our attacks were made as opportunity arose: when word reached us of something that we could exploit, we acted.

Our enemies were the enemies of Poland – both the Germans and the Soviets – and everything we did was designed to antagonize them and drive them off. As the Germans retreated, the territory they abandoned was taken over by the Russians – sometimes the mounted Cossacks, whose raids among the villages were horrific. Stories and speculation flew. It was rumoured that German officers, especially SS officers, were beginning to desert, to strip off their uniforms and insignia like so many snakes shedding their skins. Some, it was said, went so far as to wear the yellow Star of David and try to blend in among the Jewish freedom fighters, but they were easily tested for authenticity: none of them could recite from Torah. All over Poland, the forests echoed with executioners' guns.

I knew members of our fighting unit had assassinated Nazi officers, stolen weapons, made bombs, executed collaborators. I knew this. I understood that I was participating in death. I can't say how I reconciled it with everything I had done before, with all the pains I had taken to protect lives. But I did. From time to time, I would look across the campfire while we cooked our meagre dinner in the forest. Perhaps I would see Jerzy spit on a whetstone and sharpen his knife – the knife he used to cut sausages – and know without being told that he had used the same knife on a man. Or I might see Aaron study the map of a nearby town, and know that he was planning a backstreet ambush. And the memory of a baby thrown into the air would flood my mind, hurtling me down into darkness, and I would think, Yes, sharpen your knife. Sharpen it. Lay your traps.

This atmosphere of danger and defiance in which we existed made us alive like nothing else. We lived in the forest, and our senses were as sharp as wild animals'. The biting smoke from our campfires, a glimpse of a bluebell in the woods, the sudden flicker of bird wings across our path, the voices of our friends singing patriotic songs – these things all struck us so intensely that we sometimes wept with emotion. We were very young. We were fighting for our country. We were in love.

One day in early April, I was made an official member of

the partisan group, in a ceremony in the forest. Father Tadeusz, a priest who was our ally, performed the ritual in the church of the trees. I swore a blood oath to protect my country, and the priest blessed me and christened me with my new partisan name, Mała, the Polish word for little. They decided I should not carry a gun because I went into town so often; I was given a capsule of poison, however, and I solemnly swore to kill myself if I was captured by the Germans or the Soviets.

Afterward, Janek and I walked along a stream that was lined with yellow, starlike flowers. Sunlight glanced off the water onto Janek's face.

'I know I should not be happy,' I admitted, twining my fingers through his. 'Our country is still dominated by our enemies. My family is far away. And yet I am happy.'

'Happy with me.' Janek turned me to face him, and put his hand under my chin. 'Mała, my little bird, I know exactly what you are saying, because it is what is in my heart, too. I love you. I want to marry you.'

I pressed my forehead against his heart. 'I want to marry you, too.'

We returned to Kielce that evening to tell his parents. The Ridels were overjoyed at our news, and urged us to set a date. We settled on May 5, my birthday, which was just under a month away. That evening, I could barely look at Janek across the dinner table: I was afraid that my emotions would overpower me if our eyes met. I had been accustomed to hiding my true feelings for a long time. It was hard to believe that I could be happy.

Our group continued its guerrilla war as the spring turned green, but I took time out to indulge myself as a bride. On May 2, I was at the Ridels' house, standing on a chair while Janek's mother pinned up the hem of my wedding dress.

'You'll look like an angel, Irenka,' Pani Ridela exclaimed with a mouth full of pins. 'Just like an angel.'

Through the sheer curtains I saw Janek striding up the front steps; a moment later, the front door burst open and he charged in, catching me around the waist and swooping me off my perch.

'Janek!' I screamed, beaming down at him and trying to push away. 'I'm full of pins!'

'It's bad luck to see the bride in her dress before the wedding,' his mother scolded.

He put me down and swept my hair away from my face. 'We don't care about superstitions, do we, darling? I had to see you!'

'Why?' I laughed, blushing and smiling and fussing with my dress.

'We just got word – a German transport is moving through the forest tonight. We're going to hit it. We need the ammunition. It'll be a sweet little liberation.'

My stomach lurched. 'Don't go, Janek. Let someone else do it.'

'But, sweetheart! I'm the fearless leader,' he teased me. 'I'll be back before morning. I'll bring you breakfast in bed,' he added, whispering in my ear.

I giggled, but I was trying to be serious. 'Janek, please! I don't want you to go.'

'Sorry, my darling. It's all settled.' Janek was already on his way out the door. He stopped and blew me a kiss.

And then he left.

Janek was killed in the ambush. We buried him in the forest.

I wanted to die. Several times, I took the poison capsule from the little coin purse where I kept it. I would place it on the pillow of my bed in the Ridels' house and rest my cheek beside it, looking at it. I only had to swallow it to be reunited with my love. That knowledge gave me the only peace I could find in those days.

I returned to the forest, and Father Tadeusz talked with me day after day, bringing me step by step out of the darkness that clung to me. The notion of God's will had almost lost its meaning for me, I had seen so many people die during those war years. But this good priest reminded me time and again how often I had prevailed, how many times my luck had been almost miraculous; he reminded me that although many had died, many now lived because of me. That was God's will, Father Tadeusz told me. God has his reasons for everything, and we cannot know what those reasons might be.

It was heartbreaking to think that God had his reasons for letting Janek die, heartbreaking to think that God had his reasons for showing me happiness and then snatching it away from me. I could not fully accept it. But I did not kill myself. After all, I reasoned, I was a guerrilla fighter and a spy. My life might end very soon without any encouragement from me.

So I threw myself into my work for the partisans with even greater passion. I had lost all fear of death. I will not say I was reckless, but I had no hesitation. I was all over the countryside that spring and summer on my bicycle, delivering messages, delivering money. One afternoon, as I walked out of the forest, a German patrol stopped me and asked where I had come from. It was no effort at all to lie to them, to say that I had been afflicted by an 'intestinal crisis,' and had run into the woods to relieve myself. They laughed so hard they only waved me on, not even bothering to ask for identification. Another time, as I wheeled my bicycle across a guarded bridge, an officer stopped me and flirted with me. I used my best German on him, flirting back, promising to return after I visited my mother. Meanwhile, a wrapped parcel containing thousands of British pounds lay in the basket between the handlebars. I played with my golden hair as we spoke, knowing that he would stare at it, and he never even noticed the parcel. On other occasions, when we had quantities of weapons or ammunition to deliver, several of us dressed ourselves in peasant clothes and drove a great hay wagon with the guns buried in the hay. If we were stopped and questioned, I always smiled at the officers, and they always smiled back. In my heart, I was seeing them dead. But on my face, I was an open invitation.

If you are only a girl, this is how you destroy your enemies.

Flight

I lived this way through the summer and autumn, and by December, as 1944 was dying, I succumbed to pneumonia from camping in the forest and driving myself to exhaustion. Some of my friends took me into Kielce, to the Ridels'. Janek's parents wept to see the condition I was in, and being together only reminded us of our loss. We mourned even as they nursed me back to life. I was very ill for three months, and when I finally recovered, I learned that all of Poland had been turned over to the Soviets. We had been 'liberated,' whatever that meant.

The Red Army was now pouring like a lava flow toward the heart of Germany. The Battle of Berlin pounded that city into ruins, and on April 30, 1945, Hitler killed himself in a bunker far below his blasted capital.

Hitler was gone. The Nazis were gone. Poland was 'free.' But I was tired. I had no more strength for fighting. I wanted my mother. It was time for me to start looking for my family.

The Ridels begged me to stay with them, but they understood my longing. They scraped together as much cash as they could, and I left Kielce and its bittersweet memories behind me. As I began travelling across my battered country, I noticed signs posted everywhere in Russian and

Polish urging the partisans to surrender. There was no longer any need to stay hidden; the guerrillas should hand over their weapons and return to society and be welcomed as heroes.

I had not lived through six years of war to fall into such a blatant trap. I had no doubt that anyone so foolish as to turn himself in would be imprisoned or worse. I remember standing on a sidewalk reading such a notice on my birthday, on May 5. I was twenty-three, but I felt a million years old, and sometimes I was so tired I simply wanted to lie down on the street and never rise. Still, I had no intention of crossing paths with the Soviet Red Army again.

So I kept my head down. Travel was difficult: the roads and railways had all been damaged by war, and getting from one city to another could take days instead of hours. There were hostels available – everyone was on the move – and finding a place to spend the night was not so hard. Often I simply slept on a bench, in a train station, in a park. As I crossed the landscape, seeing my country in shambles, I began to understand more fully what had been done to Poland. Word spread about what the Allies were finding in the countryside, about the scale of the Nazis' extermination camps. So many little towns had been defiled by the Nazis: Oświęcim would be forever cursed as Auschwitz; Rogoźnica would be remembered as Gross-Rosen; Sztutowo would be hated as Stutthof; and the towns of Treblinka, Bełżec, and Sobibór had not even a Nazi-given German name to hide behind. Poland had been turned into the land of death. We who travelled across it in those days felt that we walked on graves wherever we stepped.

I first went to Radom, which was only 80 kilometres from

Kielce. I was overjoyed to find my aunt Helen; she had re-married, and was content to start anew in Radom. But my joy quickly turned to disappointment: she had heard nothing from my family since sending Janina back to them. She was convinced they were no longer in Kozłowa Góra. Now I did not know where to turn.

I did learn something encouraging, however. By visiting the resurrected synagogues in Radom, I learned that many Jews from the Ternopol area had migrated to Kraków. With so many lives disrupted, the ghostly survivors were drift-ing to the great cities, hoping to find their lost loved ones congregating there as well.

And so I went south to Kraków, back through Kielce again. I wanted to find my friends, if possible, before I con-tinued west in search of my family. Perhaps I was afraid of the inevitable truth: that I would not find my family. So I haunted the temples and synagogues of Kraków, reciting names: Haller, Silberman, Wilner, Bauer, Weiss. At last I was rewarded: I found Fanka.

She was working for a tailor. When I entered the work-shop, she was bent over an old army coat in her lap, ripping the seams apart with a little knife. My breath stuck in my throat.

'Fanka,' I whispered.

She glanced up, puzzled, and then sprang from her chair, dropping the coat and knife. There was a moment when we only stared, and then we were clinging together, weeping and laughing. 'Irene, Irene,' she gasped, clutching the fabric of my dress in her fists as she pressed me against her. I could not speak at all.

At last, when we were able to compose ourselves, we sat

at Fanka's worktable and tried to catch up with our news. interrupting each other, laughing from sheer giddiness – and, when I told her of my lost love, crying a bit together.

'And truly, everyone else is here?' I asked, holding her hands in mine.

She smiled. 'Well, most of us – we are practically a club. The Morrises, of course; Rosen; the Bauers, too, although I think they will return to Germany. And Wilner is here,' she added.

I squeezed her hands. 'Do you know, I always thought he liked you?'

Fanka blushed. 'Maybe he does.'

I couldn't help laughing. 'We'll see. And Ida and Lazar? Please tell me – the baby?'

'The baby was born at Pasiewski's. It's a boy, fine and healthy. His name is Roman.'

This news hit me like an electrical shock. I felt – I felt as though that baby were my baby, and that all I had endured was for his sake. Through all the dreadful things that had happened, I had brought forth this baby. I had to thank God. I could not do otherwise.

'I have to see him. Where do they live?'

Fanka's smile faded. 'Oh, I'm sorry, Irene. They're not in Kraków. They're in Katowice.'

I chewed my lip, thinking. 'That's only about sixty kilometres from here, isn't it?'

'Yes – but you'll stay for a while, won't you, Irene?' Fanka pleaded. 'Don't leave us so soon. Everyone will want to see you. And you look so tired.'

'I have been sick,' I admitted, suddenly noticing how weak I felt. The excitement of seeing Fanka had drained me.

'I'll stay awhile, but then I want to see the baby, and find my own family.'

Fanka leaned forward to kiss my cheek. 'I know, Irene. I understand. We'll help you – you know we will.'

The next few days were filled with reunions, as I met up with one old friend after another. I felt like a mother hen who finally has all her chicks together again, and I would look around the dinner table with a delighted grin on my face. They fussed over me and spoiled me as much as they could, calling me their saviour, their deliverer, showing me off to their new friends. When I finally, reluctantly, said I must resume my journey, they gave me a purse of money to help me on my travels.

Only sixty kilometres from Kraków to Katowice – and yet it took two days to get there, through endless delays and detours. Finally, I made my way to a temple and asked the rabbi if he knew Ida and Lazar. At first, he greeted me with cold suspicion: I looked so German. But the moment I gave my name, he let out a shout of amazement and threw his arms around me. 'You are Irene! Of course I know who you are!' And he led me outside, pointing out the way to the Hallers'. Once I had their address, I wasted no time in hurrying there. My mind was racing with excitement, and so many dreams of their baby's future filled my head that I noticed nothing around me.

That is why I did not see the two Soviet military police-men who had been following me. I was caught completely off guard when I was arrested.

Perhaps I should have put the Kielce area far behind me, because our partisan group had operated all over that part of southern Poland. But the lure of seeing that baby boy was too much for me to resist. As it was, for someone whose name meant little, Mała had a big reputation from Kielce to Kraków. Not only was I recognized, I was suspected of being the leader of the partisans!

The interrogations went on for days. Often, when I had been taken back to my cell and had fallen asleep, I would be dragged awake for more questioning. I denied everything. I had been well schooled in deception, and the Soviets got nothing about the partisans from me. Since my interrogation in Ternopol so long ago, I had become a champion liar, and I thought I could hold out against these new questions.

All I told them, over and over, was my name, my hometown, and the story of my cruel enslavement by the Nazis – of the destruction of my honour when I was made the concubine of a German officer. Every indignity, real and imagined, that could befall a poor helpless Polish girl at the hands of the wicked Germans: this was the story I poured out to the liberators of my homeland. I swear, no actress could have put on a more convincing show of wronged innocence and ignorance than I.

And yet they were not convinced.

Day after day went by in this way, and I began to despair; perhaps my miraculous luck had at last run out. Then, for no reason that I could understand, they decided that I needed a new kind of humiliation. I was made to work during the day, scrubbing floors and cleaning toilets, while my nightly interrogations continued. I was exhausted. If I had still had my poison capsule, I might have used it. I was afraid I would grow too confused, and be unable to keep up my pretence, and that I would endanger my comrades.

'Who were the other partisan leaders?'

'Where are they now?'

'How did you communicate with London?'

'How many did you command?'

'How many weapons do you have stockpiled?'

'What acts of sabotage are you planning against your liberators?'

'What are the names of the other partisan leaders?'

I concentrated on a picture in my head: not one of Mamusia or Tatuś – their faces brought tears and made me weak, as did the faces of my sisters. Not one of Janek – no, not Janek. I pictured Bociek, the stork we had rescued as little girls, that wild, mysterious, frightening bird. Even wounded he was formidable, jabbing with his dagger beak, his shiny, black eyes blinking at us in defiance. We kept him in our cellar all winter, feeding him frogs, fish, mice – anything – and hoping to tame him. But he would not be tamed. When spring arrived and his wing was healed, he flew away the moment we opened the door and did not return.

'Who is Bociek?' my interrogator asked quietly.

I was alarmed. I did not realize I had spoken aloud, but when he leaned forward, eager, and asked again who Bociek was, I could not stifle a small laugh.

'He was a stork,' I said, feeling renewed strength as I giggled. 'We found him with a broken wing and we made him better. Mean old Bociek. He stabbed my hand with his beak once. I thought it would get infected, but it didn't. You see?' I held out my hand; it didn't even tremble.

'Take her away,' the man said in disgust.

Luck was with me still. One morning, I was taken to the second floor of a wing of the prison. I noticed that the bars on the hallway windows were spaced far enough apart for someone as small as I was to squeeze through. I was told to enter a particular room to clean it, but when I went in, I found ten or fifteen men – guards, I suppose – in the process of getting dressed. They looked around at me in surprise as I let out a gasp.

I flung my bucket and mop down, furious and embarrassed, and ran out of the room. As the door slammed shut behind me, I found myself in the hallway – alone – beside an open window. Without thinking, I hoisted myself up onto the sill, squirmed between the bars, and dangled for a moment, gripping the clammy iron rails between my hands. And then I let go.

By the time I'd limped my way to the Hallers' apartment building, my feet were swollen like melons. I knew I had not broken any bones – thank God – but I must have broken several blood vessels when I landed. I had run on adrenaline, searching for the Hallers' street. 'Find Ida,' a voice whispered to me. 'Find Ida.'

I propped myself up in the doorway, examining the list of names alongside the buzzers. My hand shook as I reached out to touch the button labelled 'Haller,' and as I waited I squeezed my eyes shut and breathed shallowly, trying to master the pain in my feet and ankles. From somewhere nearby came the sound of a piano. Chopin.

At the sound of footsteps from the foyer, my eyes flew open. The door handle rattled, and I was staring at a Russian uniform.

'I – I am looking for the Hallers,' I mumbled, darting a frantic look to the street for an escape route.

'Are you Irene?'

I stared at the soldier. 'What?'

'I'm Finix, Haller's brother-in-law. Don't be misled by the uniform. I wore it to fight Germans. Come in.'

I tried to take a step, but my knees buckled. Finix picked me up as easily as if lifting a cat, and carried me into the building. Stars swam around my vision as my feet banged against the door frame. For a moment, I thought I would faint.

'We heard you'd been arrested – the rabbi told us you were on your way here, but when you didn't show up, we asked around. How did you get free?' he asked.

We were going down into the basement. The stairs were lit by a weak bulb. 'I jumped from a window – that's how I hurt my feet,' I whispered. 'Are Ida and Lazar here?'

'Yes. You'll be safe down here for a moment while I get Ida,' Finix said, setting me down and propping me against the wall like a rag doll.

I looked around me in wonderment as he went back upstairs. I was being hidden – in a basement laundry room! I had time to hobble to the sink, where I was able to hitch myself up off my feet. Then I heard footsteps clattering down the stairs, and Ida ran toward me.

'Irene! My dear! I'm so glad you're safe!' she cried, wrapping her arms around me and holding me tight.

I held her just as tight, pressing my face into her shoulder. 'Must we always meet in cellars, Ida?' I don't know if I was laughing or crying.

'Oh, Irene! God must have his jokes.' She, too, was laughing – or crying.

'Ida! I had to see you and Lazar and your baby, but the Russians . . .'

'I know, Irene. We have to get you away from here right away. To Kraków . . . Finix is bringing a car. He'll take you somewhere safe.'

I pushed back so that I could look into her face. 'But your baby, Ida. Can't I see him before I go? Is he healthy and strong?'

Her face crumpled. 'Irene, every night I ask God to bless you for making me keep my baby.'

'But can I see him?'

'If we have time,' Ida said, glancing at the doorway. 'How are you?'

'I'm alive. I'm here.'

She winced. 'Yes. A complicated question, perhaps. But—'

Finix stuck his head into the laundry room. 'Ready?'

My heart sank. Even as Finix came to pick me up again, I grasped Ida's hand.

'God blessed you with a family. Help me find mine, now,' I begged. 'They were living in Kozłowa Góra, in Oberschlesien. Can you help me? I won't be able to travel freely if the Russians—'

'Anything, Irene. We'll find them.' Ida kissed me one more time, and then Finix carried me back upstairs, out the door, and into the backseat of a car, where he covered me with a blanket.

I recuperated for two weeks in the care of Moise Lifshitz and his wife, Pola. They told me they had been in the

Ternopol ghetto, and had escaped after one of my early warnings; now they were anxious to repay me. Word from Katowice was that I was wanted by the Soviets as a dangerous criminal, and was being hunted throughout the area.

Meanwhile, the grapevine of Jewish survivors who were putting their lives back together was busy on my behalf, asking friends, who asked other friends – these questions found answers that nearly killed me. The first was the news that my father had been killed by the Germans several months earlier, shot for failing to step off the sidewalk at the approach of two drunken soldiers. And on top of this, I learned that my mother and sisters had been arrested by the Soviet secret police because of me, the dangerous fugitive partisan. I had kept my partisan friends safe, only to bring danger to my family.

I lay in my bed, staring at the ceiling for hours, as tears ran down past my temples and soaked the pillowcase. For years, I had kept myself going with the hope that someday I would be reunited with my family. Now even that hope had been taken from me. I had brought the loss on myself.

Sometimes, while I looked dazedly at shadows in the corners of my room, I could not believe that I was still alive. Not that I had survived so many physical dangers, but that I had taken so many wounds to my heart and was still living. I was ready to turn myself in, to exchange myself for my family, but more news reached us: my family had been released, and had gone into hiding. No-one knew where they were. Their only safety lay in disappearing. I could not seek them out without putting them in danger again. I had to give up my search.

There was nothing for me in Poland now. But where could I go? I was at a loss: I was finished with fighting, but I had forgotten how to do anything else. For many months, my friends sheltered me in one place or another – they let me heal, let me gather my strength. But my idleness was terrible, because it gave me time to think, to remember. And always, there was this question: where could I live without fear?

On German Soil

My friends gave testimony on my behalf to their rabbi. A copy of this document remained with the Jewish Historical Committee in Kraków, and the other was given to me as my passport to a new life, whatever that was to be. I had no idea what to do or where to go, and whole days would pass when I could not shake myself from the fog that clouded me. I did not know Irene.

At last, it was my friends who took charge of me, who made me one of them and then sent me onward. They knew the Allies were creating repatriation camps for displaced persons all over Europe. For millions of people uprooted from their homes, whose towns had been destroyed, whose lives were blown to the four winds, these camps were a refuge. Food, shelter, medical care were there in abundance; schools and loving attention for orphans; immigration officials to assist people in finding new homes across the seas. The camps were for Poles and Hungarians, Latvians and Italians, Ukrainians, Gypsies, Serbs, Dutch, for all the displaced people of Europe – but most of all for the Jews. The shattered, the hunted, the haunted Jews. I would be one of them.

We dyed my hair black. My friends gave me a transit pass with a Jewish alias, Sonia Sofierstein, and put a ticket in my trembling hand. And then I boarded a train for

Hessich-Lichtenau, Germany. To seek shelter in Germany, disguised as a Jew, was only one more bizarre irony. I had grown accustomed to this strange sense of humour fate showed me.

There had once been a time – in my girlhood – when riding in a train was a happy adventure, when I would watch my fellow passengers and try to imagine the reasons for their journeys – to show a new baby to the grandmother, to meet a fiancé's parents, to enter university, to go on holiday, to go home. Now, on a train that click-clacked over the trestles and made the black pine boughs sway and shudder, it was impossible to imagine such things. We were all escaping.

I asked myself what I was escaping from. Not just the Russians; no, it was more than that. Sometimes – maybe when I turned my head just so and caught a glimpse of something as the train rushed through the wooded landscape – sometimes I saw a baby being thrown into the air and shot like a bird. When this happened, my heart would pound in my chest and a scream would rise in my throat and I would cry out to myself, Will I see this forever? Will I ever escape this vision?

I saw this same question in the faces of the people who shared my compartment on the train. Their deathly stares, their pallor, their painful thinness, their silence – these were the evidence. It must be that each of them relived one scene over and over, just as I did: the moment a body fell to the ground; the moment an aged parent was sacrificed; a moment of betrayal, a moment of dreadful understanding. We were all doomed to remember.

I watched through the window as the scenery fled past

me. It was May 1946. Another birthday had come and gone, and nearly seven years had passed since my happy world had ended. Where was I headed? Where could I land?

My arrival at the DP camp in Hessich-Lichtenau did not provide an answer, as I had hoped. Everyone there was turned inward. Some seemed sedated, like sleepwalkers. Children played only quiet games and moved in silent packs, like animals on the prowl. They had grown up in a universe that did not make sense, and some of them were almost completely feral. They mistrusted any tenderness.

Once I had identified myself to the rabbi, shown my documents from the Jewish Historical Committee, I was welcomed as a hero and could shed my alias. I was anxious to be useful, to find a place where I fit in. I began to work in the camp infirmary, struggling to recall the rudimentary lessons from my distant nursing-school days. I was busy. I made friends. I fooled myself that I belonged.

A group of young, strong people, men and women, arrived at our camp. They were outdoor people, tanned and fit, who spoke Hebrew with their own accent. They were Jews from Palestine, and they called themselves Israelis. Their organization was called the Haganah. 'Come, fight for Israel, a new state,' they said, touching people on the shoulder, pointing toward the south-east.

But before I could decide if Israel was the place for me, I succumbed to diphtheria. Once again, I was sick for many weeks, and my recovery took months. When I was well again, the doctors told me that the disease had changed the rhythm of my heart. I was unfit for Israel. The Haganah needed strong bodies, and now I was useless to them. In my weakness, I would hear the young survivors at their Hebrew lessons and be filled with despair.

Somehow, months went by. I had been well over a year at the camp. All around me, people were coming back to life. The beauty of the countryside healed our spirits even as our bodies grew stronger. Our camp in Hessich-Lichtenau was a community of survivors. Our holidays became more joyous. People laughed. Many moved on – to Palestine, back to their home countries.

I had made a place for myself in the village, and I lived there for three years. But still, it did not feel like home. And then, in the summer of 1949, a delegation from the United Nations arrived to interview survivors. Rabbi Stern found me in my room, reading a letter from Ida.

'Irena, there's someone here I think you should talk to. I think he'll be interested in your story.'

I folded the letter back into its envelope and followed the rabbi to the dining hall. There, a tall man in horn-rimmed glasses sat at a table, a briefcase open before him. The rabbi waved me forward. 'Irena Gutowna; William Opdyke,' he said with a nod toward the UN delegate.

Mr Opdyke smiled as he rose, and held out a chair for me. I sat opposite him, watching Rabbi Stern as he left the room.

'Hello. How do you do?' Opdyke said. He spoke in English.

'*Dzień dobry. Czy pan mówi po polsku?*' Do you speak Polish? I asked.

'Hmm. *Parlez-vous français?*'

I shook my head. '*Sprechen Sie Deutsch?*' I tried.

He shook his head. I tried Russian. I tried Yiddish. We

had six languages between us, but not one in common – except the language of laughter. We could not help chuckling at the predicament we were in. He called across the room to a colleague, and in a few moments we had another American with us, one who spoke German.

Through the interpreter, I told Mr Opdyke my story. He interrupted a few times to ask questions, but for the most part he let me tell my story as the details came to me. Some of it was out of order, sometimes I had to pause to collect myself, but by the end of an hour, I had told him the essential elements. I left nothing out – I think I wanted to shock him, to tell this well-fed American what a simple Polish girl was capable of.

Opdyke had been taking notes, but he finally just put his pen down and stared at me. For a moment, I feared that he did not believe what I had told him. He said something to the interpreter in a gruff voice.

'Mr Opdyke says he feels honoured to have met you, and that the United States would be proud to have you as a citizen.'

'Me? America?'

Opdyke extended his hand, and I shook it, while we both nodded solemnly at one another. 'America,' he repeated.

America.

Amber

What had happened to me through those years? How had Irena Gutowna become that person? Like a fledgling pushed from its nest, I had been forced to learn how to fly. I looked down as though from a great height, viewing the wreckage of Europe below me — the ruined grain fields, the cratered roads with their endless lines of refugees toiling onwards, the smoking towers. Nothing was clear. At the war's end, there was no time to say what must be said, and no time to see what must be seen. We flew from it, and did not wish to see it, and closed our mouths to keep our griefs in.

But now I look back as an old woman, and with one old hand over my brow to shield my eyes from the glare, I receive my past. I can see myself and I can speak. Yes, it was me, a girl, with nothing but my free will clutched in my hand like an amber bead. God gave me this free will for my treasure. I can say this now. I understand this now. The war was a series of choices made by many people. Some of those choices were as wicked and shameful to humanity as anything in history. But some of us made other choices. I made mine.

Sometimes, still – often, still – I cannot see myself in the mirror; instead, as if through a haze, I see a baby thrown into the air. But I will myself to change this vision. Something is thrown up into the air, yes, but it is a bird, it is a little bird released from a cage, and it flies away, rising higher and higher over the treetops, and over the roofs of the houses. A young girl leans out a window to *scatter crumbs and watches this bird until it disappears from view. It is a little bird flying. A sparrow soaring.*

This is my will: to do right; to tell you; and to remember.

Z Bogiem. *Go with God.*

Postscript

Late in 1949, Irene saw the Statue of Liberty from the deck of the troopship *John Muir*, which carried refugees from Europe. She was greeted by a member of the Jewish Resettlement Organization, who found her a place to live in Brooklyn. Before long, Irene was employed in a garment factory and learning English. Her new life had begun. Then, one day, to her astonishment, she bumped into William Opdyke in a coffee shop near the United Nations.

He remembered her vividly – how could he not? – and began to court her. They were married a few months later. Five years after her arrival at New York harbour, Irene became a United States citizen. She and Bill had a daughter, whom they named Janina, and they lived among the orange groves of Southern California, in the sunshine, in a place untouched by war.

Because the Soviet Iron Curtain had sealed Poland off from the West, it was difficult for her to hear news of the family and friends she had left behind. But bits and pieces reached her. She learned that Major Rügemer had been ostracized by his family because of his involvement with Irene and her friends, and that he had been cared for in Münich by the Hallers until his death. Many of her friends had emigrated to Israel, where they started new lives in the Jewish homeland. Sadly, she also learned that her mother had died shortly after the war's conclusion. With no end in sight to the Communist control of Poland, she feared she would never see her beloved sisters again.

Like many refugees from the war, Irene tried to put her experiences behind her. But when she began hearing that some people here in the United States believed the Holocaust was an exaggeration, a propaganda myth to promote support for Israel, she broke her silence and began to tell her story. She speaks to church congregations, to synagogues, to community groups. Her favourite audience is high school students, because she wants especially to convince young people that they can make a difference, that they have the power to fight against evil.

In 1982, Israel's Yad Vashem Holocaust memorial recognized her heroism and honoured her as one of the Righteous Among the Nations. On her trip to Israel for this ceremony, she finally met Roman Haller, the baby – now a grown man – whose life she had made possible.

And with the end of the Communist regime in Poland, Irene returned to her homeland in 1984 for the first time since the war, and there met Janina, Marysia, Władzia, and Bronia, and their families.

Polish: A Rough Guide to <u>Pronunciation</u>

Some Polish consonants look like English consonants but are not pronounced the same way. Some consonants don't look like anything we're used to.

'Ł' is pronounced almost like an English 'w' sound; thus 'Mała' is pronounced 'Mawa.'

'W' has an English 'v' sound, so 'Wisła' is pronounced 'Veeswa,' and 'Gutowna' is pronounced 'Gootovna.'

'J' is pronounced like English 'y,' so 'Janówka' is pronounced 'Yanoovka.'

'Ch' has a guttural sound, rather like a cross between the English 'k'and 'h.'

'Dz' sounds like an English 'j', so 'dzień dobry' (hello) is pronounced 'jen dobry' and 'dziękuję' (thank you) is pronounced 'jen-kooyeh.'

'S' sounds like English 'sh,' so 'Tatuś' (father or daddy) is pronounced 'ta-tush'.

'Ż' sounds much like an English 'zh,' so 'dorożka' (wagon) is pronounced 'doe-roe-zhka.'

Vowels in Polish can be pronounced more or less as English speakers pronounce them, with the exception of the letter 'ę' as in 'Częstochowa.' This letter is pronounced with a nasal tone, so that the name of this city sounds like 'Chenstohova'. Other Polish vowels, even with unfamiliar accent marks, can be intelligibly pronounced like English vowels.

'Pan' and 'Pani' are Polish for 'Mr' and 'Mrs'.

German: A Rough Guide to <u>Pronunciation</u>

German consonants differ somewhat from English.

'S' before a 't' is pronounced 'sh,' making 'Strasse' (street) sound like 'Shtrassuh.' Otherwise, 's' at the start of a word is pronounced like English 'z,' making 'Sagen Sie' (you say) sound like 'Zagen zee.' A double 's' is pronounced like an English sibilant 's,' as in the example of 'Strasse.'

'W' is pronounced like English 'v,' as it is in Polish, giving us the sound 'Vahrenhouse' for 'Warenhaus.'

'Ch' is pronounced as a guttural in the back of the throat, a throat-clearing sound.

'Sch' is pronounced 'sh.' 'Scharf' (sharp) is pronounced 'sharf.'

'J' is pronounced like 'y,' so that 'judenrein' sounds like 'yoodenrine.'

'Z' is pronounced 'tz.' 'Schulz' is pronounced 'Shultz.'

Vowels in German are more or less as in English, with some exceptions.

'E' at the end of a word is always pronounced as an 'uh' sound, so 'bitte' (please) is pronounced 'bit-uh,' and 'danke' (thank you) is pronounced 'dank-uh.'

'Ei' is pronounced like the long English 'i.' 'Meine' (mine) is pronounced 'my-nuh.'

'Eu' is pronounced 'oy.' 'Heute' (today) is pronounced 'hoy-tuh.'

'Äu' is also pronounced 'oy.' 'Fräulein' (Miss) is pronounced 'froy-line.'

Some Historical Background

Some of the terms used throughout this book may be unfamiliar.

In 1939, when Hitler's army invaded Poland, they moved the German-Polish border to the east, annexing a large part of western Poland (including Kozłowa Góra). What remained, called the General Gouvernement, was a Polish state controlled by Germany under the strictest martial law; the greatest number of concentration camps and death camps were in the General Gouvernement. The explicit policy of the General Gouvernement was the subjugation, enslavement, and eventual eradication of the Poles in order to create *Lebensraum*, or living space, for the German people. Polish nationals living to the west of the new border (like Irene's family) were likewise subjected to the harshest domination by the Germans. Władysław Gut's murder for failing to yield the sidewalk to two soldiers is demonstration of that.

Many people today assume that all Germans involved in World War II were Nazis, but the Nazi party (Nationalsozialistische Deutsche Arbeiterpartei) was a political institution, which not everyone joined. However, membership in the Nazi party was usually a prerequisite for

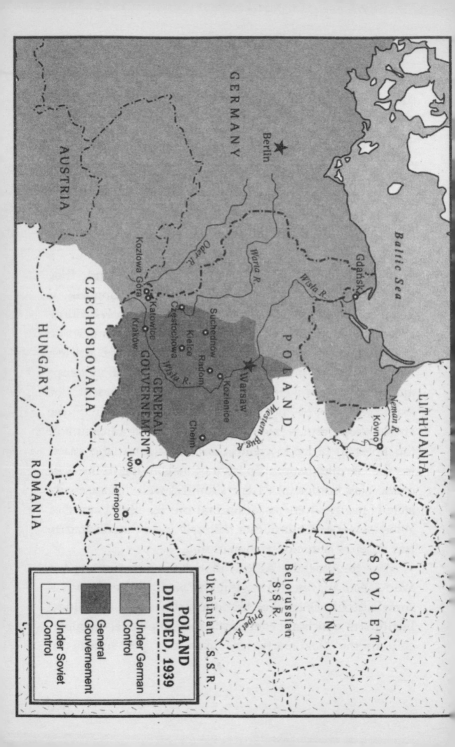

POLAND
DIVIDED, 1939

Under Soviet
Control

General
Gouvernement

Under German
Control

advancement in the German army, and many army officers who did not necessarily embrace Hitler's politics nevertheless became Nazis to promote their careers. Therefore, Major Rügemer was a member of the Nazi party, but Schulz apparently was not.

The Germans exerted control in Poland in two ways: militarily and politically. The military, the German army, was the Wehrmacht. Wehrmacht soldiers were not always Nazis. The Schutzstaffel, or SS, was the political police arm of the Nazi party. The Wehrmacht conducted the war; the SS made up Hitler's elite personal guard and conducted terrorist and police actions, such as the deportation and extermination of the Jews and other political 'enemies' of the Nazi state. The Gestapo (Geheime Staats Polizei, or Secret State Police), originally a separate Nazi organization, had been taken over by the SS before the beginning of the war. Thus, many people used the terms 'SS' and 'Gestapo' interchangeably.

Rokita was an officer of the SS; Rügemer was an officer of the Wehrmacht. These two groups, the Wehrmacht and the SS, had different command structures, and often worked at odds with one another; while the Wehrmacht needed labour to supply its military operations and made use of Jewish slaves, the SS was devoted to Hitler's goal of Jewish extermination. Thus, Major Rügemer and Rokita had different and conflicting aims.

After the war, the Allies redrew Poland's borders yet again, restoring much of western Poland but assigning a large part of eastern Poland to the Soviet Union. Today, Ternopol is part of the independent country of Ukraine.

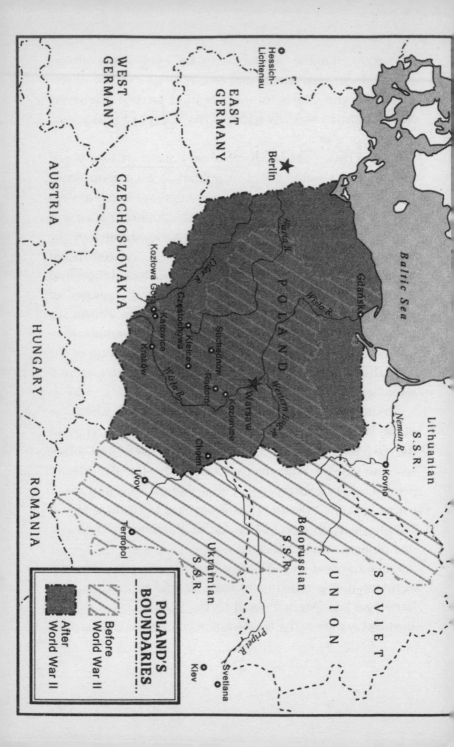

POLAND'S
BOUNDARIES

▓ After
World War II

▨ Before
World War II

▫ ▫ ▫

WEST GERMANY

EAST GERMANY

Hessich-Lichtenau

Berlin ★

AUSTRIA

CZECHOSLOVAKIA

HUNGARY

ROMANIA

Kozlowa Gora

Katowice

Kraków

Częstochowa

Kielce

Skarzysko

Radom

Kozienice

Chełm

Lvov

Ternopol

Warta R.

Oder R.

Wisła R.

P O L A N D

Wisła R.

Western Bug R.

★ Warsaw

Gdańsk

Baltic Sea

Neman R.

Kovno

Lithuanian
S.S.R.

Belorussian
S.S.R.

S O V I E T

Ukrainian
S.S.R.

U N I O N

Pripet R.

Svetlana

Kiev

A Note on the Writing of This Book

The events of this narrative were told to me by Irene Gut Opdyke through many, many hours of interviews. They have also long since been verified and confirmed by Yad Vashem: the witnesses gave their testimonies; the survivors have spoken. This is a true story.

There were some details, however, particularly names, that Irene couldn't remember. You must bear in mind that these experiences took place many decades ago and, for the most part, under extreme conditions. You can't always recall every conversation you had, or the name of every street you walked on, or every person you met over fifty years ago when you were in fear for your life. So there are some few instances where I have taken the licence to invent, to imagine how a scene might have played out, or to supply a name typical to the situation. Irene encouraged me to do this, to help make her story come alive.

That being said, however, rest assured that these characters – Irene and her family, Dr Olga and Dr Miriam, Major Rügemer, Sturmbannführer Rokita, Schulz, and of course, the Jewish survivors whose lives Irene saved from the Holocaust – are real, and this is what happened to them. As I sat in Irene's home in Yorba Linda, California, listening to her speak, I found myself shaking my head in wonderment. This sweet, blue-eyed grandmother, who welcomed me into her home, who fed me pierogis, cookies, and mangoes from the tree in her backyard – this woman had done things I could not imagine doing. And here she was, in spite of it all, full of love, full of charity, full of hope. I was afraid to write this book, to put myself into her past. I was afraid to pretend to be Irene, because I fear I can never live up to her stature.

If I have done justice to this story, I am grateful. If I have not, it is because I have never had to face what Irene has faced. I am known as an author of historical fiction, and my job is to make fictional events bear truth, to imagine the reality. The few things that I did invent for this narrative do that, I hope. They are there to describe the truth of the events, even when they don't record the facts precisely as they transpired.

In the end, though, as much as I fervently wish these terrible and brutal events so typical of World War II were fictional, they are not. Irene does live with the image of a baby thrown into the air and shot; she will have to live with that image for the rest of her life.

But fortunately for humankind, the good and heroic events she recalls were typical as well. And they are true, too.

Jennifer Armstrong